RUNNING WITH ZOÉ:

A CONVERSATION ON THE MEANING OF
PLAY, GAMES, AND SPORT

Including: A Journey to the Canadian Arctic

John Kilbourne, Ph.D.

AuthorHouse™
1663 Liberty Drive
Bloomington, IN 47403
www.authorhouse.com
Phone: 1-800-839-8640

First published by AuthorHouse 7/28/2009

ISBN: 978-1-4490-0846-8 (e)
ISBN: 978-1-4490-0845-1 (sc)

Library of Congress Control Number: 2009907351

Printed in the United States of America
Bloomington, Indiana

This book is printed on acid-free paper.

FOR ELIZABETH, ZOÉ & PARKER

MY PARTNERS IN PLAY, DANCE,
GAMES, SPORT, AND LIFE…

TABLE OF CONTENTS

PART ONE

RUNNING WITH ZOÉ:

A Conversation on the Meaning of Play, Games, and Sport

PART TWO

A JOURNEY TO THE CANADIAN ARCTIC   87

* * * * *

Chapter I

Origins of a Journey

———◆———

The world itself becomes a habit in no time at all. It seems as if in the process of growing up we lose the ability to wonder about the world.

- Jostein Gaarder

IT WAS AN EXTRAORDINARY DAY, June 2, 1983. I was poised on the rear of a large flatbed trailer that was being pulled down Broad Street in Philadelphia. Standing next to and around me were several players and their families from the 1983 National Basketball Association World Champion Philadelphia Seventy-Sixers. Other coaches, players and Seventy-Sixer administrative staff were on similar flatbed trailers that preceded and followed ours. Yes! I was part of this great basketball team that was celebrating after having reached the Promised Land.

At the beginning of the 1982-83 season I had been hired by the Seventy-Sixers as the first full-time strength and conditioning coach in the NBA. Now, after a successful regular season (65 wins & 17 losses) and a nearly perfect post season, we were the 1983 World Champions of Basketball. As the parade crept through the heart of Philadelphia rejoicing fans surrounded us. Some estimates were that as many as one million, five hundred thousand people participated in this tribute. Broad Street was absolutely wild. People were literally hanging from

1

the windows of skyscrapers. Folks of every age group and of mixed ethnicity were waving and screaming with ecstasy. A few folks actually took their clothes off and were rejoicing naked. It was unbelievable, to say the least.

It was somewhere during the journey down Broad Street towards Veterans Stadium that I asked myself, what is this all about? Just what is this phenomenon we call sport? And, what has sport done to these folks to cause this many to celebrate in ways never seen, heard, or felt, at any other time or place in my life? There had been many moments in my life where I thought I had reached the height of human expression and spirit. As an adolescent I sat with my father and brother at a *Doors* concert in Sacramento, California, and watched Jim Morrison dance and sing in ways unimaginable to a fourteen year old. As a teenager I witnessed several demonstrations and concerts in the San Francisco area. These were the great Peace-Love-Music festivals of the late 1960's and early 1970's, *Jimi Hendrix, Janis Joplin, Country Joe and the Fish.* And, as an amateur and professional actor/dancer I had performed on stage, hearing and feeling the cheers of appreciative audiences. One high point of my calling to the stage was performing with The American Ballet Theatre in the Ballet *Petroucka* at the Dorothy Chandler Pavilion in Los Angeles. Also, in 1980 as Graduate Assistant (Dance Conditioning) to then Head Basketball Coach Larry Brown at U.C.L.A., I was part of a team that went to the N.C.A.A. Final Four Championship in Indianapolis, Indiana. As spectacular as all of these life experiences were, none were even close to what I was feeling on this electrifying June morning. The celebration in Philadelphia was downright orgasmic. Ecstasy of the highest order. It was during the Seventy-Sixers' parade that I began my quest to understand the phenomenon of sport. This revelation and the ensuing crusade originated more than twenty-five years ago. During that twenty–five years I have continued sharing information about dance, movement and conditioning with college and professional basketball players and teams, worked extensively with American and Canadian figure skaters, and remained active in the theatre and dance arenas. Most importantly, I have been a devoted sport philosopher, thinking about and trying to understand the nature and conduct of humans and their participation in sport. Although much closer than I was twenty-five years ago, I still seek answers to the many questions I have about play, games and sport. *Running with Zoé* are my reflections at this juncture of the crusade. The chapters of the book are a progress report on my journey towards an understanding of each. It is my hope that by sharing my journey you will become closer to understanding the deeper meanings of play, games, and sport. Our nearness may help bring society into greater harmony with the values that are inherent in the games we play.

Sport and American Folks

Modern sport is one of the most watched, participated in, read about, and listened to events of our time. This certainty was demonstrated by the fact that nearly one-hundred million Americans watched the Super Bowl in 2009. Despite sport's popularity, those in sport and those who observe sport know little if anything about the deeper meanings of sport.

I began to ask questions of myself and others about the meaning of sport after my revelation during the Seventy-Sixers' Championship Parade in 1983. To my surprise, those that I questioned at every level and from a variety of sports, primarily coaches and players, were as naive as I was. The naiveté seemed most apparent amongst the elite and professional athletes with whom I was working. Most of them had no concept of the influence sport has over people, both past and present, in our society.

It was while working in the arena of college sport that I uncovered one possible reason for our lack of understanding about sport. During my doctoral research at The Ohio State University I discovered that there was not one American college or university participating at the elite level of college sport (Division IA) who required their student-athletes to take a single academic course that would enhance their understanding of sport, i.e., sport philosophy, sport history, sport sociology, or sport psychology. It seems that over the years organized education has created a culture of sport participants; team owners, administrators, agents, coaches, players, parents, journalists, marketers, and spectators who know very little about the meaning of sport. Thousands of young athletes pass through schools, colleges, and universities throughout America and then advance to play sport, administer sport, coach sport, report on sport, sell sport, or watch sport, without any insight into the meaning of sport for individuals or communities.

This lack of understanding concerning sport is evident in every arena of sport, from youth sport to professional sport. It is reaffirmed almost daily as we witness the personalities, behaviors and deportments of team owners, team administrators, coaches, athletes, parents, agents, television announcers, and marketers. We are all too familiar with the pandemonium that surrounds sport, from 250 million dollar, guaranteed, ten-year player contracts (One player's annual salary equals the salaries of 750 entry level school teachers), to the legions of parents who loudly and sometimes violently protest coaching and referee decisions. *Running with Zoé* is my attempt at trying to enliven the wonder of play, games, and sport. My hope is to help the sporting public understand the deep meanings of play, games, and sport. I have purposefully created a book that can be easily understood by the popular sport culture. Play, games, and sport are a *People* phenomenon. Creating a work that is only understood by an esoteric few would have little impact on the future of the games and sports we play.

Chapter II

A Conversation with the Canadian National Figure Skating Team

Go fish and hunt far and wide day-by-day, farther and wider, and rest thee by many brooks and hearth-sides without misgiving.

- Henry David Thoreau

CHAPTER II IS A CONVERSATION I had in July, 1994 with the Canadian National Figure Skating Team. I was invited to deliver the keynote address at the team's annual training seminar. The team consisted of the forty finest figure skaters in Canada, young men and women ages sixteen to twenty-five. The conversation was a participatory event. The skaters were all invited to share and assist with the discourse. Together we explored, and reflected on, the origins and meaning of games and sport.

The Origins of Games

John K. - Good evening and thank you, ShaeLynn Bourne, for that very sincere introduction. It is always a pleasure to visit Canada and share with Canadian figure skaters. Today we are going to talk about where games came from and why games and sport are here? Towards that end, I am going to ask each of you to participate in our discussion. Most of you already know the answers to these two questions. During our conversation I would like each of you to become contemporary philosophers, that is, I want you to begin to think about human nature and conduct as it relates to games and sport.

In order for our dialogue to be meaningful it will be important that each of us help create a safe environment. If, for example, I ask a skater to come up to the front, put on antlers and act out the life world of a moose, we all must support his/her moose-like efforts. To facilitate meaningful understanding we must all be able to extend ourselves and moreover, be comfortable taking risks. So, can we all provide for a safe and supportive environment for our fellow athletes? (Heads nod in approval; some skaters say yes, the French speaking skaters say Oui!). Okay! Let's together, begin our voyage towards an understanding of games and sport. In order for us to determine where games and sport came from, we must look to the past and attempt to discover why folks have been involved in games since the beginning of time. And, when I say that we must look to the past I am not talking about the Ancient Greeks or Romans. We must go way back, 5,000 to 20,000 years. What do you think games of this early period looked like? Can we, by uncovering the intention of games during this time, shed light on the meaning of games and sport today? What are the common denominators that exist between early games and contemporary sport? If similarities do exist, are their meanings the same for men and women who are involved in, and witness sport, today?

Now is your chance to help in our exploration. What do you think was the first game? Anyone can speak. There are no wrong answers.

Male Skater - *Sex! (Everybody laughs).*

John K. - Good answer! There is some logic to what you have said. The game or sport of sex however, is a another lecture. Can we, for the time being, keep the game or sport of sex stored in our bodily beings until later. For now, put it aside and take yourself back 20,000 years and think about what folks might have been doing for games?

Male Skater - *Hunting!*

John K. - Yes! And what did they hunt?

Male Skater - *Women! (Skaters chuckle and laugh).*

John K. - Oh, you again. I can see that some of us are having trouble setting *Sex* aside. Now seriously, why did these early folks have to hunt?

Male Skater - *To live!*

John K. - So, our first games were a survival mechanism. And what did these early games provide for folks?

Female Skater - *Food and clothes.*

John K. - And, what else?

Female Skater - *Bones.*

John K. - Bones for what?

Female Skater - *Tools.*

John K. - Yes! Exactly. Our early games were linked to survival. From our early games we obtained food, clothing to protect ourselves from the elements, bones for weapons and tools, and animal fat which was placed in lamps to illuminate and heat our surroundings. Early tribes or communities would send their best hunters (athletes) into the wild for days at a time in the hope that they would return with the nourishment, clothing and tools necessary for survival.

Hunter/athletes of this early period were primarily men. It was not that women did not possess the skills to be successful hunters. Quite the contrary. The evidence shows that women certainly had the talents to be successful hunters and in some areas of the world they indeed were as accomplished at hunting as their male companions.

Ancient tribes' folks however, needed the unique capabilities of women for another highly specialized task. And what do you think, was that specialized task?

Female Skater - *Children.*

John K. - Yes! What can women do for children that we men will never be able to duplicate? Sorry guys. We are simply inferior when it comes to this important task.

Male Skater - *Have them.*

John K. - You're right again! Women most certainly give birth to children. We, as men, will never be capable of doing this. And then after giving birth, what do women provide for the young offspring?

Male Skater - *Food!*

John K. - Yes! Women possess the abilities, both physical and emotional, to nourish the young children of the community. And, this important function was not finished in a matter of weeks or months. Early women nourished the young of the community for up to three or four years. Of all mammals the human requires the longest period of nurturing before we can survive on our own. It is because of their unique abilities that women needed to remain close to the tribe or community while the men traveled in search of food, clothing, and tools. Women struggled to raise and safeguard the young children while at the same time managing the community household. Women were also accomplished gatherers who provided a majority of the sustenance. Without the unique abilities and skills of women our species would have been doomed. Games for women were very different, and certainly as important, as games for men.

The activities that men and women performed provided a great deal of stability for these ancient tribes and communities. It was a simple, equitable division of labor. The men were more proficient at throwing, and debilitating large animals; while women on the other hand, were masterful at providing sustenance for, and nurturing, children. There was little competition between men women because each understood their reciprocal relationship. Together they formed a harmonious team. Where do we do our modern hunting and gathering?

Male Skater - *The grocery store!*

John K. - Yes! When I go to the neighborhood grocery store I often tell my wife and family that I am going hunting and gathering. (The skaters chuckle and laugh). Moreover, technology has made it much easier for women to share the nurturing of our young with men and others in the community. Not having to remain close to the home to nurture the offspring, modern women are free to participate in the efforts that make contemporary hunting, that is, our weekly visit to the grocery store, possible. In other words modern women, like modern men, go to jobs that provide the means for survival.

The only thing we require to be good philosophers is the faculty of wonder.

Jostein Gaarder

Now, where were we? Oh yes! We were at the point of becoming an ancient tribe or community. Let's pretend that we are all part of an ancient tribe or community. Some of you are ancient men, some are ancient women, and others are young boys and girls. Our tribe has not eaten any meat in two or three weeks. The young boys and girls need new shoes and many of our tools are falling to pieces. What are we going to do?

Male Skater - *Go hunting...*

John K. - Correct! And what might we do before we send our hunter/athletes into the wild?

Female Skater - *Have a going-away ceremony.*

John K. - Why would we want to do this?

Female Skater - *To wish them (the hunter/athletes) Good luck.*

John K. - You're exactly right. We know from anthropological discoveries that prior to the athletes' departure on their hunt, the tribe's folk would gather in ceremony. This celebration served to unify the tribes' beliefs and practices relative to the sacred (religion). It provided the tribe with a connection to the task at hand, that task being survival. During the celebration, which included music, dance, and drama, the tribe's folk would ask higher powers for success and abundance during the hunt. Often times the athletes of the tribe would actually create a pre-hunt drama about the ensuing search. They would visibly share with their higher powers and the community their anticipated success. This pre-hunt, pre-game drama was very much akin to pre-game pep rallies of today. For thousands of years community members, men and women of all ages, have gathered to cheer and encourage athletes with music, dance, and drama. Like these early folks, we continue to unify our communities with pre-game tributes to athletes in the hope that they will achieve success for themselves and insure the survival of the citizenry. These early hunter/athletes might have been gone for several days or weeks. When they finally returned to the community, what were the reactions of the tribe's people? Yes, go ahead and show us your reactions.

Skaters - *Faces light-up in excitement and bodies shift and move with ecstasy.*

John K. - Right! That is exactly how earlier folks reacted. Everyone was excited when the hunter/athletes returned from their journey. The members of the community would soon rejoice in festive celebration. These celebrations would include a ceremonious meal of the rewards from the hunt, libations and, more music, dance, and drama. During the celebration the hunter/athletes would actually reenact the events of the just completed hunt. Let's see if we can recreate this festive performance. I need four or five hunter, huntresses to come up-front.

Yes, huntresses! This is a new generation! Women are accomplished hunter/athletes. (Three skaters come forward immediately, two more move to the front hesitantly).

Okay! We want you two (one male and one female) to put on these animal head-dresses and you three (two males and one female) to ready yourself for the hunt. Here are your hunting weapons. (Each hunter/athlete is given a decorated badminton racket). Now, we will send the animals with the head-dresses over to this side of the performance arena and the hunter/athletes will move to the other side. Now, we want you to reenact the events of your recently completed hunt. Go ahead. You are on your own... (The other skaters rise out of their seats to witness the events of the game performance).

Skaters - *The five athletes begin to move towards each other while improvising the events of a hunt. The spectator skaters laugh and howl with approval. To and fro, over and under, back and forth, above and below, the hunter/athletes struggle to be supreme over their foe. Finally, after an engaging performance the skaters disengage their prey. They have their trophies...*

John K. - Thank you very much. That was extraordinary! Let's show our approval of their success with a nice round of applause (Skaters show their appreciation with cheers and whistles). Thanks again. You may return to the tribe...

The event you have just witnessed is a re-creation of an early game performed for a spectator audience. Ancient hunter/athletes would actually adorn themselves in the hides and headdresses of the prey over which they had struggled to be supreme. They would then share with their fellow tribe's folk the circumstances of the hunt. Their game performance furnished the community with a myriad of uplifting, meaningful, activities and lessons. What do you think were some of these activities and lessons?

Male Skater - *Entertainment!*

John K. - Just what do you mean by entertainment?

Male Skater - *You know, it was entertaining. It was fun.*

John K. - You're correct! However, entertainment and fun are lavish words. They can mean many things to many different people. Let me see if I can help you. First of all, these entertaining and fun game performances provided the people of the community with opportunities to re-direct their inborn physicality. They were exciting movement experiences.

Human folks are, and always have been, physical beings. The very act of learning and memory begins with the movement of the young embryo in the woman. Humans re-direct their physicality at the micro level in the synaptic connections in the cells of the brain and, at the macro level, in the fine and gross motor movements of the human body.

Game performance, together with the men's hunting activities and the women's gathering/nurturing activities, provided the means whereby tribe's people could re-direct their inborn physicality. What were the other lessons that the community gained from the game performances? Physical expression was most certainly one. What is another?

Female Skater - *Communication!*

John K. - What do you mean by communication?

Female Skater - *It was, kind-of, you know, how they got to know each other.*

John K. - She is correct. A very perceptive huntress/athlete. Very good. Wow! You see, the physical expression displayed in these early game activities and celebrations was, for these folks, a primary form of communication. Lacking sophisticated language or writing techniques, it was through their physical actions that the tribe's people began to communicate with one another. Moreover, it was through these physical dramas that they began to learn about themselves, their beliefs and practices, and the environment. Cooperative bonds were formed that would serve to solidify the community and safeguard everyone's future. Again, games served as a survival mechanism.

Now, there is still one other major lesson that was derived from these early game performances. Can anyone think of what that lesson might have been?

Male Skater - *Were these hunters also teachers? Maybe they helped to teach the kids?*

John K. – Yes, Yes, Yes! Very good again. You see, I told you earlier that you had all of the answers. Last and most importantly, these early ritualistic game dramas would assist in teaching the young of the community. It was through moving with and imitating the games of the adults, that young boys and girls would master the knowledge and experiences they would need as mature citizens. Yes, game participants were, and always will be, role models. Basketball great Charles Barkley and Nike Shoes, Inc. are wrong when they say otherwise.

I am sure that you are all aware of Charles Barkley, the outspoken National Basketball Association superstar who stated rather emphatically in a Nike Shoe television commercial that, "I (athletes) am not a role model." Well, Charles is wrong. However, we should not hold Charles Barkley or Nike Shoe's, Inc. entirely responsible for their ignorance. Unfortunately, they are the products of a culture that has failed to teach those in games and sport, anything about games and sport. They have never been asked to think about human nature and conduct as it relates to games and sport. They have never re-created an ancient game performance. Like many in sport, Charles Barkley and Nike Shoes, Inc. are unsophisticated when it comes to understanding the deeper meanings of the games we play.

My own spirit was opened to the notion of games as a teacher during my tenure with the Philadelphia-Seventy Sixers Basketball Team. On this team we had an exceptional athlete/hunter/teacher, the virtuous Julius, *"Dr. J"* Erving. Let me share with you one of his extraordinary lessons.

During one of our road trips to the west coast I was fortunate to be teamed-up with three Sixer players, Julius, Bobby Jones, and Clint Richardson. On long road trips three to four team members would often be provided with rental cars from one of the team's advertising sponsors. On this particular day we were in Los Angeles getting ready to play our west coast rival, The Los Angeles Lakers. It was a week-day and the team had gone to The Great Western Forum for a game day shoot-around. Following our practice every player, except Julius, returned immediately to the hotel to rest-up for the evening's contest. Julius had agreed to do an interview and remained after practice. He asked if I would stay with him and together we could drive back to the hotel. Without hesitation, I agreed. (When you are in the presence of an athlete/hunter/teacher of Julius' caliber you rarely have other things to do. There is no greater feeling of hope for the future). After his interview we got into our rental car and I attempted to back out of the tunnel that leads to the Forum. As soon as we felt the sunlight from the sky overhead, approximately fifteen to twenty young, multi-ethnic children surrounded our automobile. I am sure that each had skipped school with the hope that they could see one of their heroes. With us inside, our rental car was enveloped by a sea of energetic humanity. Many athletes would have startled these young children and then sped away. Julius however, in his own extraordinary way, asked me if I had anything to do. He said he would like to talk to these children for a few minutes. I immediately answered Julius saying, "That would be fine." Julius and I both got out of the car and I watched as he proceeded to talk with these young folks while at the same time signing each of them an autograph. There were no fees for his services and no autograph agents taking their percentage. Most of the children wanted his autograph on the side of their dilapidated and soiled sneakers.

Without hesitation Julius obliged. To these young folks this may have been the most important day in their lives. Some of these children may no longer even be alive. For a brief moment, a moment that will most likely last forever, they had felt the presence of a human who reassured their hope for survival and gave them a promise of a better tomorrow.

The next time a young person asks you for an autograph or wishes to shake your hand after they shower you with flowers and other mementos, think about the virtuous *"Dr. J"* and the millions of hunter/athletes who, over thousands of years, have graciously fulfilled their responsibilities as teachers. These hunter/athletes are the reason our civilization has survived.

For thousands of years games have provided persons of all ages with meaningful activities and lessons. Games provided opportunities for humans to re-direct their inborn physicality, to communicate and cooperate with other humans and the environment, and they served as a classroom where the youth would master lessons important for their future and the survival of their tribe/community.

Games were one of our earliest teachers. The athlete's performance was an affirmation that tomorrow would be a better day. The struggle for success over the environment and nature, both animate and inanimate, provided human beings with faith and hope. Simply stated, games were intimately linked to our survival. This is where our games, and ultimately modern sport, came from. This is why you, the present generation of hunter/athletes, are here. Your contribution to the tribe/community is most significant. Please do your best to preserve for the next generation, the precious jewel of game and sport performance that past generations of hunter/athletes have passed on to you.

Thanks for your help in making our voyage back through time a success. You give me great hope that tomorrow will indeed, be a brighter day. Thank you.

Skaters - *Skaters stand and cheer wildly in appreciation...*
Personal Reflections on the Conversation

To truly understand modern sport one must realize that the games we play still satisfy our basic needs of re-directing our physicality, communicating with others and the environment, and cooperation. Games are, and always will be, a human drama about our struggle to be successful. We struggle in games because we want to have consummate control over our bodily beings. We struggle in games so that we can enjoy harmonious and exemplary relationships with others and our environment. These are the universal truths of games. When it comes to game performance it seems that the more we have changed the less we have changed. Despite the fact that we no longer have to hunt or gather to survive, we still must satisfy our fundamental needs of re-directing our inborn physicality, communication, and cooperation. Games, just as they have done for thousands of years, continue to satisfy these needs.

The game and sport dramas of today are intimately linked to the dramas of long ago. Humans of all ages continue to adorn themselves with costumes (uniforms) and headdresses (helmets & hats) and engage in contests to test their physical supremacy and communicative capacities. The *Forty-Niners* struggle against the *Rams*. The *Warriors* struggle against the *Timberwolves*. The *Braves* struggle against the *Blue Jays*. And, the *Bruins* struggle against the *Red Wings*.

Contemporary athletes and teams at every level resemble ancient game participants. Modern games, like ancient games, are a reminder of the fertility and survival significance of the gaming experience. Through ceremonious physical struggle, modern game participants share with other humans the hope for renewal and survival.

Games today are also a struggle to communicate and cooperate with disparate people and groups. Success in games has always been dependent upon cooperative bonds with other humans. Early game participants had a marvelous respect for their fellow game participants. It did not take them long in their struggles for survival to figure out that the whole was more effective than the sum of the individual parts. Their every day existence was dependent upon the community unifying in belief and practice. This is a lesson that would benefit many in our modern games and sport. Today, with the transformation of many athletes into private, egocentric, micro-corporations we often witness selfish individual play rather than selfless team play. Nowhere is this transformation more obvious than in professional basketball.

The game of basketball can be a magnificent team drama. At its finest, basketball is like good jazz music. Five people play their physical instruments and the synchronicity of these individual instruments moving towards a common goal produces a beautiful and harmonious symphony of movement. Today, what we witness all too often in professional basketball is no longer the synchronicity of players but detached solo athletes whose only concern is their individual statistics and endorsements. These same athletes would have had little chance of survival in earlier times. Only time will tell if our games as they are presently played will continue to survive in the future. The pre-game celebration, game, and post-game celebration were also the means whereby ancient communities came together in belief and practice relative to the sacred; the same can be said of games today. Many have characterized our modern games and sport as, the "People's Religion." Throughout history our games have been linked to religion. It was through our games that humans first began to look to higher powers for comfort and hope. Early communities were unified in the belief that powers beyond their control would favor the hunter/athletes and safeguard the future of the tribe.

Our games continue to facilitate connections between humans and higher powers. People gather in sacred places (Arenas, Parks, Fields), at sacred times (Olympics, Superbowl, The World Series, and March Madness) and join in fellowship with other people and nature. Together they witness Supreme Beings (Athletes) achieve virtuosity beyond what was thought humanly possible: The hail Mary catch in football, the sixty foot jump-shot in basketball, the World record in track, the quadruple jump in figure skating. Modern audiences then observe the victors raise their heads and arms to the almighty and give thanks for their glory, while the defeated look to higher powers to provide comfort during their loss. Throughout history the liturgy of our games (a repertoire of ideas, phrases, or observations) has provided people and communities with the hope that tomorrow will be a better day.

One of the many wonders of our games is how you can be almost any place and, through games, enter into a union with others. The bond is more penetrating than race, gender, socio-economic status, or religious conviction. Together through games, disparate people can become *One* in belief and practice. As a former resident of Detroit, Michigan I would often marvel at the separatist residents of Bloomfield Hills (a wealthy superb north of Detroit made up largely of white people who have abandoned the predominately African American City of Detroit), sitting in their private luxury boxes in the Palace of Auburn Hills in Michigan. These folks would cheer-on the predominately African American Detroit Piston basketball team. For one brief moment, a moment in game performance, these diverse people were united in belief and practice; they were "One." Early game participants also had a sacrosanct admiration for nature and the environment. It was from nature and the environment that these ancient folks secured the nourishment that would maintain their survival. They knew that without a positive, reciprocal bond they were doomed. Modern games still remain linked to nature. We play on green grass with wooden bats and leather gloves, we swim in clean rivers and lakes and we hike up tall mountains breathing fresh, clean air. For many, our earliest connections with the environment are a result of our play, games, and sport. Through our games, we learn to respect and appreciate clean air, unpolluted rivers and lakes, and plants and animals in their natural habitat.

People will always find outlets to satisfy their universal needs of re-directing their physicality, communication, and cooperation. If not provided with positive outlets, folks of all ages will find their own negative outlets. They will re-direct their physicality through misdeeds and violent crimes. They will communicate and cooperate with other humans in surrogate tribes known as gangs. They will associate with nature in ways detrimental to our environment and our future. Early game participants had little choice of how or where their universal needs would be satisfied. Their needs were intimately linked to their survival and likewise their participation in games. These early folks did not enjoy the luxuries of supermarkets (food); hardware/lumber stores (tools/shelter); malls (clothing); electricity (light); televisions, C.D Players, cellular telephones, facsimile machines, computers, e-mail, or the World-Wide Web (communication). For thousands and thousands of years people have satisfied basic human needs through game performance. Over the years games have provided human beings with near absolute satisfaction. Any cultural phenomenon with a history of fulfillment as complete as games deserves our complete understanding. It also deserves our commitment to make it as meaningful and affirming today, as it was in ancient times. The games we play may possess the greatest number of available possibilities for us as a society (tribe, community) to re-direct the physical energy, that is destroying many persons and families, build constructive and meaningful relationships between our disparate groups and strengthen our relationship with the environment. Appreciating these truths of our games, truths that have been validated and tested over thousands of years of history, is long overdue.

We participate in games because we have always participated in games. Game performance is tightly woven into the fabric of our bodily beings and our lives. These threads can never be removed. Through our continued participation in, and viewing of games, we seek the means whereby our universal needs are satisfied.

Chapter III

A Conversation with Richard Nelson

Exploring the Near at Hand

———◆———

Health depends on a state of equilibrium among the various factors that govern the operation of the body and the mind; the equilibrium in turn is reached only when man lives in harmony with his external environment.

- Hippocrates

Prologue

DR. RICHARD NELSON HAS DEDICATED most of his adult life to understanding the relationships that exist between the traditional people of Northern Alaska and their environment. For more than twenty-five years he has lived with these First Nations peoples and written about their shared life world. His approach is one of participation, not observation.

"Exploring the Near at Hand," is an interview Dr. Nelson shared with, *Parabola: The Magazine of Myth and Tradition.* With permission it is included in *Running with Zoé* to reveal the reverence the Northern Alaska First Nations people have towards traditional games. The reverence these people share is the same reverence that has accompanied games for thousands of years. Understanding traditional

nature and conduct in and through games and sport may foster greater understanding about games and sport from modern day participants.

Reprinted from PARABOLA, Where Spiritual Traditions Meet.
Volume XVI, Number 2, Summer 1991

Richard Nelson spent twenty years as an anthropologist working with Native peoples in Northern Alaska and studying with Koyukon elders there. His most recent book, *The Island Within*, (which is being released in paperback this month by the Vintage division of Random House), examines these life experiences for a more general readership, focusing especially on The reciprocal relationship between mankind and nature. We (Rob Baker and Ellen Draper) recently had a lively and enthusiastic exchange in Parabola's Manhattan offices.

PARABOLA: In your book, The Island Within, you speak of "becoming fully involved with the near at hand." All too often, most of us seem to ignore the ordinary, everyday aspects of life, failing to see their relationship to a greater whole, to the laws that govern our universe. The metaphor you use is your own search for meaning within the confines of a small, uninhabited North Pacific island. Can you say how this "becoming fully involved with the near at hand" on that particular island relates to a respect for the universe at large and a continuing search to understand and relate to it in a deeper way?

RICHARD NELSON: I think in the Koyukon way – or at least what I understand of it – the moral and ethical principles that guide and restrain you in your relationship to the world extend beyond the enclave of humanity. In our western tradition, law is pretty much restricted to our fellow human beings – to our family and the members of our community. But for Koyukon people, and I think for traditional people all over the world, this web of legal and moral obligations extends all the way out, to everything that exists in the world around.

And so my teacher, a Koyukon woman named Catherine Attla, said, "There's a really big law that we have to obey." She compared it to the Supreme Court for non-Native people. And she said, "That law is respect. We have to treat everything with respect. The earth, the animals, the plants, the sky. Everything." What enforces that law is the world itself, not other humans. So for a Koyukon person, if you mistreat a part of the natural world – if you're disrespectful toward it, if you don't approach it with humility and restraint – you suffer, you pay consequences. That can be through personal suffering or illness, or you can lose your luck, or something bad can happen to you. So in the Koyukon way of seeing the world, the enforcement is always around you. As one old Koyukon man said, "There's always something in the air that watches us," meaning that everything we do, no matter where we are, whether there are people around or not, we are always subject to these rules, because everything around us is aware of what we're doing.

P: Let's take one concrete example from the first chapter of your book, about hunting a deer. What laws are involved there?

RN: For me – the way I understand the teachings of Koyukon people and the way these rules impinge on me when I'm hunting – first of all, it means to speak and think respectfully of this animal. Even here, in New York City, far away from my home, I wouldn't say something disrespectful about any animal back where I live. I would try not to behave in a way that was arrogant, or that in some way set myself up as superior to anything in the world where I live. And in hunting, there's a sense of approaching the animal with right-mindedness: that what you're doing is something delicate and powerful and profound, that you come to this place asking an animal for its life, and in a sense, asking it to grant you yours, or to become a part of yours. That's the most important gift you could ever ask of anything – to be part of your life. When I'm hunting, if I kill an animal, that's when I feel the most powerfully obligated to that animal: to use all of it that I can possibly use. There are parts that you leave behind, part of the inside, and the head. I always say something when I do that, that that is left for other animals; it's sort of a sharing. When you remove the animal's body, and you're doing things with it, when you take it home and hang it up and work on it, for example, you always need to be very careful where you do that.

Mostly I hunt alone, but sometimes I hunt with other people. And I never hunt with someone who I think might be disrespectful in some way. I'm very, very careful. There are very few people I would hunt with. I have to know a lot about a person before I would go, because I think it wouldn't be right for me to hunt with someone who in his own way didn't show respect. I don't care if it has anything to do with my way, as long as there is respect.

I don't know what kind of spirit and power and awareness might exist in the natural world, but I feel I should behave as if it's there. So the matter of knowing is less important to me than the matter of respect. Making some kind of daily gestures of respect towards your source of life keeps you mindful of where you come from. By doing all these little gestures, saying "thank you" to people, saying "excuse me" treating friends and community members with respect, we remind ourselves that we belong to a community and we need each other. We make these gestures to keep the bonds between us strong.

P: Why is that relationship based on respect so necessary?

RN: Because there is this constant reciprocity. We are inclined to treat people kindly because we are in direct, reciprocal relationship with them at all times. If I mistreat you, I'll find out about it right now. But as a culture we have created a kind of distance between ourselves – a physical distance, of space – between ourselves and what keeps us alive. And so we forget, we become a really forgetful people. We've forgotten that we are just as dependent on the environment as a pygmy or a Bushman or an Australian aborigine, or an Eskimo or an Indian living in a traditional way. We are as much a part of nature as they are. The only difference is, we forget.

P: What about that moment of confrontation between the hunter and the prey? At one point in the book, you are about to shoot a deer. Then you realize that she has a fawn with her, so at the last moment, you don't shoot. That moment seems very much the same as the moment when you do finally shoot another deer, only your action is different. Can you describe those two moments?

RN: One of the really important focal points of my life is to find moments of intensity and intimacy and closeness with animals. I don't know why that is. For me there is very little difference between moments when I only watch an animal and moments when I am hunting – they are part of the same thing, in the sense of a complete focus of mind. There are a few times when I'm out in the woods walking all day long hunting, and it's as if no time had passed. If my mind is really focused that way, it's like a walking meditation. But then when I'm hunting and I meet an animal. There are decisions to be made on both sides. The animal may stay there or the animal may leave; that's something you take as it comes. But then there are other moments, when the decision is yours. Probably ninety-five or ninety-nine percent of the time, I make the decision not to hunt an animal. I don't know exactly what the reasons are. But when I make the decision to hunt an animal, it's usually really early, when I've first seen it. At that time, it's almost as if another mind clicks in. As I expressed it in the book, the mind that loves to watch animals shuts off, and the mind that hunts animals – and loves them in the hunter's way – turns on. From that point onward, it's just like a whole different way of thinking. It's incredibly elemental.

That emotional part of me, the bird-watcher, isn't there anymore. Once I've made that decision, I don't engage in ambivalence.

P: You talked about the focus. Is the focus narrow and direct, on the animal, or is it a kind of wider focus, so that, for example, you did notice the fawn that time, out of the corner of your eye?

RN: The thing I remember, especially from living with Innuit people, is that they never completely focus their attention on one thing, because to do that is dangerous. You have to remind yourself, if you're approaching an animal as a hunter, to always look around for something else that might be going on. On the island, that something else is most likely to be a brown bear. You could find out that you're not the only person who's interested in that deer, or that the deer is not the only person who's interested in you.

Also, as one of the stories in the book emphasizes, when it's a doe, you have to be extremely careful not to kill the animal who has a young one. Young ones very quickly become independent of the mothers, in the sense that they only take milk for a short time, six weeks or so, but they follow them around until the next spring. I don't want to interfere with that.

P: There must be a great difference between hunting for sport, and hunting for survival, for food, the way Native people do, and the way you do when you're living on the island.

RN: For me, the number one thing that's in my mind in hunting an animal is that this is for my food, and that I'm doing a very difficult thing in order to stay alive – that it's not a game, and I am not the person who has the power out here. I've heard some sport hunters talking back and forth, and they speak in ways that I won't even repeat, because of the arrogance and the disrespect for animals. There's a big power thing going on. One of the deep teachings in the Native American tradition is always to try to rid yourself of the impulse to feel power: to remember that the power is out there, the power is not in you.

P: You referred before to how we all have a certain relationship with the world. Even people who live in New York City have a relationship with nature, without knowing what that is, exactly, or on what level. How could a person, living in this city made of concrete, learn the kind of lessons that you've been able to learn because you were so immersed in nature itself?

RN: As I was saying earlier, it's a matter of becoming mindful that we all live from the earth, and that we are all part of the earth. And that's not some sort of a hazy saying, that's the truth. Every time we eat something, we've engaged in a direct, one hundred per cent dependency and reciprocity with the earth. The problem is that it is so easy for us to forget where the Granola and hamburger and the bean sprouts and the pancakes and the eggs and the corn chips, all the rest of that stuff came from. It's like saying grace. Gary Snyder talks about how we need a grace, like a little reminder. That's what I'm talking about with gestures of respect towards things. If people would think each time they sat down to a meal, if they would consciously remember where that food came from, I think it would be a significantly different world that we live in. If people at least once a day were aware when they drew air into their lungs that that air was a gift to them from everything around them, that that came from trees, and had gone through all sorts of other animals and all sorts of other people – if people would think of that once a day, we could be moving in the direction of a different world. That to me is the really deep wisdom of the Native American tradition – and probably of traditional cultures all over the world: that mindfulness of where it all comes from.

P: To take another example from the book, you speak about the way Native people go and choose a tree and make sure that it's the right tree, and take a long time to cut it down. How does that attitude differ from the way logging is done commercially?

RN: Among Native American people whom I've lived with, a person cuts down a tree individually. One tree. Among Koyukon people, when you do that, you've created a reciprocal relationship to that tree and you have to treat the tree in a certain way. If it's a birch tree, and you cut it in the winter, you wouldn't just strip the bark off of that tree and leave it out in the open overnight. You're supposed to cover it with snow. People say that after you use the wood from the tree, if there are shavings, you should take those shavings and put them out in the woods somewhere, not just leave them, as if they don't matter. You should put them out in the woods in a place away from a lot of human activity. There are all these gestures of respect towards that tree; each tree is treated as an individual.

When you start to cut down trees for commercial purposes, then they become a resource, they become a product. Loggers cut down thousands and thousands and thousands of trees, and not for their own use. When we do things commercially, the person who actually harvests our food for us, does it *en masse* – huge quantities every day. The fisherman kill thousands of fish, so the fish or the trees are no longer individuals, they're resources. And somehow I think that that mass engagement with things must numb life. We take whole mountainsides and wipe them completely bare of trees, and whole valleys, and take away all the trees, and the ones we can't use, we leave there, lying on the ground.

P: But isn't it a bit too easy to say that we all need to go back to a simpler way of life? It seems to me that now we have a new situation. We now have these large-scale demands on the food supply, pollution exists, there's a new hole in the ozone layer. We can't just say that it shouldn't be, because it is. Perhaps everything that is going on now is not really unnatural. Maybe it is lawful.

RN: You're right. We struggle with this idea of restoring some sort of natural condition. But what is that? One in which there are no humans? I think this is the real flaw in the whole environmental movement, and in a lot of our nature writing, our nature photography – this attitude that there's something wrong if there's a human being in the picture. For me that's not the point at all. It's not a matter of eliminating humans from the situation; it's a question of having humans integrated into a situation in a way that's healthy. You can't live in a place without changing the environment. All animals change their environment in some way.

There's another issue related to hunting. People think of a natural condition as a place in which there's no hunting. How can you say that? Human beings were here hunting for thousands of years. The whole environmental community of the entire continent was one in which hunting was integrated.

People talk about our culture as if it's unnatural and other cultures as natural. But wait a minute. That's too easy.

P: Native people don't see bad guys and good guys in nature either, do they, in such a simplistic way? The brown bear, which is dangerous, is still treated with respect.

RN: In our own tradition, not so much today as in the past, we took it upon ourselves, as part of creating a "right" community, to get rid of grizzly bears, to get rid of wolves, to get rid of mountain lions. We didn't want any predator there but us. But the Koyukon people compete directly with wolves for food, so some of the elders have said to me: "We don't think there should be too many wolves. We should hunt wolves, or we should trap wolves. But we would never want to get rid of them. Because they belong here. That would be like eliminating something that is your kin." They believe, for example, that wolves leave food for people. Wolves will sometimes kill an animal, and people come along and there it is, and they interpret that as food left for them, by the wolves.

That's a very different way of looking at things. If everything is there because it belongs there, you may change something, but you shouldn't eliminate anything. That would be a pretty big transgression. Also, that would be too much of an exertion of power.

Once I was living in Huslia, a Koyukon village, where each spring the ice on the river breaks up and moves out in a great chaos of churning spans of ice, grinding against the banks. Sometimes the ice jams up, and when it does it creates a dam and the river rises up and floods villages. So what people do when the ice is moving is go out and talk to it. They thank the ice for giving them a road to travel on all winter, and they say, "Now I hope you'll go on away easy." They're thankful, and they're sort of humble in asking the ice to take it easy with them. Then they pray in Christian ways, too, to the ice – they hold a church service next to the river.

Once when the ice jammed up down river, white men had a different way to deal with it: they brought in jet airplanes and bombed it. The people thought that was deeply wrong, because it was an assertion of power: you're not doing what we want, so we are going to make you do what we want. People didn't like that at all.

And then, for the next couple of years there were these terrible floods. People say that was because of the offense, the affront to the ice that was done by bombing it.

I thought that was a really nice juxtaposition of the two ways. One, you pray to it, you ask it to do right, and the other was, you bomb it and make it do what you want.

P: How does the central image of your book fit in with these ideas? What do you actually mean by "the island within"? And how do you use the symbol of the island itself, and its mirror image: that which surrounds it?

RN: It makes a nice metaphor because we all live on an island in one way or another. After we moved to where we live, because the island is nearby, I spent more and more time there. I became increasingly curious about my relationship to the island, especially about the way it was coming inside me in different sorts of dimensions. First, the island was so much in my mind, the way someone you love is in your mind all the time. That was one way. And in whatever nebulous way I have a sense of a spiritual relationship to the world, this island became the focus of that, for my sense of spiritual relationship to the world, for my sense of spiritual relationship to a place. And third – and this came as a real surprise to me – was the recognition that, physically, I was coming to be made out of this island. I made this conscious decision to get as much of my food as possible from the island. Venison. Fish from the waters around it. Berries. I was taking the island inside myself, as food, and so there was a sense that the boundaries between myself and this place had become less and less distinct. I know that my body is made out of that island and that something from the island flows through my body. I think that's where "the island within" idea came from.

P: In a sense, each of us has an "island within" that we can explore?

RN: Anyone can have this sense of moral and spiritual engagement with a place. One of the deep sources of that is to choose a place and focus on it in some way or another. It doesn't matter if it's in your backyard in the city, or Central Park, or a farm field. It's to find a place in which you can feel deeply engaged, and then go back to it over a long period of time. Make that your place. I think there's something very, very important about that engagement.

Coming back to the question of urban life, that engagement is something that's available to all of us. We can say, "This is going to be my place, and I'm going to take care of this place, and I'm going to try to understand my engagement with it." Another way to express it is – and I'm not sure I'll say this exactly the same way I did in the book – but "There may be as much to learn by climbing the same mountain a hundred times as by climbing a hundred different mountains."

P: Is there another island to move on to ?

RN: It would break my heart to leave.

P: Are there more books on this island?

RN: I hope so. I've started a book about deer. I'm sort of at the beginning stages of that right now. It basically will be an excuse to be involved with these two things that I love: the island and the deer. I hope to spend a year or so following deer around, at the same time studying the western and the Native American way of knowing this animal, and then to try to integrate it all into a book. But the real reason I want to do this is because I want to know more about deer: by my own personal experience, and by learning from scientists and from Native American traditions.

I think it's very important to understand what hunting truly is. We really need to understand better, as a society, what it means to be a hunter, and what the various permutations of hunting are.

P: This intense research seems to be a kind of hunt in itself. That need for careful preparation and study – it's as if the laws of nature, or writing, or any real search or effort we're involved in, require something from us in response. We have to meet them to a certain extent. We can't just glamorize going out to climb a mountain in our sneakers, for example, with no equipment or planning: it's too dangerous. There has to be a certain amount of daring and exploration, but also a certain amount of sensibleness.

RN: Knowledge is so much the key to living in a wild place. I first encountered this living with Innuit people in northern Alaska, and then with the Athabaskan Indians. As you live in a place longer and longer, your knowledge just seems to become deeper and more and more detailed. For me it's one of the most exciting things about being on the island; learning a little bit more all the time. And the more you learn, the more you realize your ignorance. My teacher, Catherine Attla, who is one of the most knowledgeable people I've ever known, points out constantly what little we know of this, what little we know of that. There is deep humility in the tradition, an idea that we can't pretend we know a lot. Part of it is that you really recognize that the world is vastly more complex, and vastly more detailed than you could ever comprehend.

That's one of the reasons why I've taken pains in my work as an anthropologist to always say as an opener that I know very little about this. And the same thing goes for the island. When I began the island book, I said, I'm going to write this book, and that implies some sort of completeness and some sort of knowledge. But I said the only way I can feel comfortable with this is to write the book as a kind of progress report: this is where I am now, recognizing that there will always be farther to go.

P: *"Becoming fully involved with the near at hand." Perhaps that's the most interesting thing of all: to want to stay and explore further, when most people would be on the next plane, to the next adventure.*

RN: Wendall Berry has a book called *Traveling at Home.* That idea fascinates me. For me, I know that I could spend the rest of my life in an area that's within a twenty-mile diameter of my home and have plenty more to explore. Right now, I can't wait to get home. The more you learn, the more you realize your ignorance.

Richard Nelson

Chapter IV

A Conversation With Zoé
Play, Games, & Sport

———◇———

Might play be the primary condition through
which the universe was created?
Might the very "work" of the universe be its play?

To run with the wind, to play with sand, to play with water are
not merely idle statements of language, but real descriptions of
what a child does when he or she encounters these properties.

Richard Lewis

MY CONVERSATION ABOUT PLAY WITH Zoé is followed by a discussion of games and sport. In my many conversations about games and sport, whether it is as a guest speaker, coach, or college professor, I have discovered that very few folks actually understand these two phenomena. Despite the fact that millions of people participate in, watch, listen to, talk about, write about, and read about games and sport, few can define them.

As you read this chapter I would like you to pretend that you're on a personal journey to understand games and sport. You can be anywhere you like. Some of you may choose to remain in the comfort of your home, some may choose to run with Zoé and I along the beach, and still others may choose to be actively engaged in other forms of play, games, or sport. Please feel free to stop reading and ask yourself questions at anytime. When you ask questions you are engaged in philosophic thought. You are thinking about games and sport and their relationships to your human nature and conduct.

The Conversation

Daddy (John K.) - *Zoé! Stop running for a minute. Look over there! Those gulls look like they are playing with each other. They almost look like they are laughing.*

Zoé - (Slowing down to a walk). Dad! Look at that big one. Do you think he is the daddy bird? He looks like an old bird.

Daddy - *You don't have to be old to be a daddy! And, that "he bird," just may be a "she bird." That might be a mother gull. Look at all of them. They look like they are using that big rock as a slide. They are slipping down the rock into the water. I have never seen birds do that before.*

Zoé - Maybe that is why they are laughing. Dad, remember the time I went down that big slide in Columbus, Ohio? Remember that boy who I played with? Can you tell me that story again?

Daddy - *Yes, I remember. You laughed just like these birds when you reached the bottom of the slide. The slide story is important because your play with the young boy and the slide helped your dad understand the many wonders of play. Your simple lesson taught me to appreciate how important play is to our life.*

Zoé - Remember that little boy dad? He was pretty silly wasn't he? How old was he?

Daddy - *You are probably about his age now, seven years old. I wonder if he still lives in Columbus and still goes to that park. I am so thankful to you and that little boy for sharing with me the miracle of play.*
(**The Wonders Of Play** *are listed here as a prelude to their discussion in our conversation. The ten wonders that are listed come from the literature and many experiences about and with play).*

The Wonders Of Play

One - Play involves movement of the bodily being.

Two - Play is a voluntary activity (free).

Three - Play involves risk.

Four - Play involves imitation of other human beings and the environment.

Five - Play involves pretending (make believe).

Six - Play involves bonding between other human beings and the environment.

Seven - Play involves alternation and change.

Eight - The product of play is only play (play is not done for profit or material gain).

Nine - Play involves a solution or resolution.

And, despite what outsiders might think or say, to the participants.

Ten - Play is a very serious activity.

Zoé Playing with the Young Boy on the Giant Slide

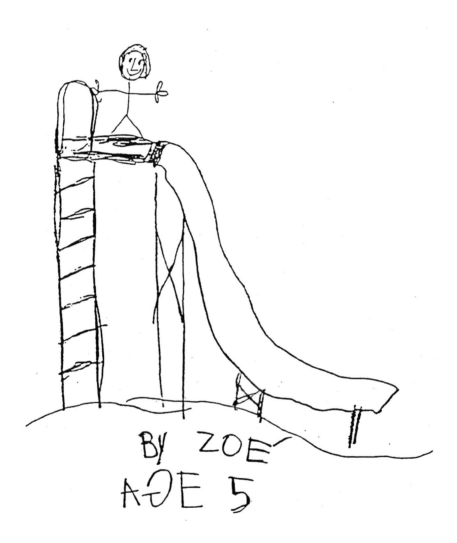

Daddy - *We were living in Columbus, Ohio while Daddy was working on his doctorate at The Ohio State University. One day when I had a morning free you and I went across the street from where we lived to play in the Park of Roses. It was a beautiful fall morning.*

Zoé - Yes, I remember. We lived in that tiny apartment and Cindy lived across the hall from us. Doesn't Cindy live in Puerto Rico now?

Daddy - *Yes, and she has a young brother. What was his name?*

Zoé - I don't remember. It was a funny name. Maybe Alvin?

Daddy - *I don't remember either. While at the park you noticed a young boy, six or seven years of age, climbing-up and swishing down a giant slide that stood in the corner of the park. You ran quickly (<u>movement</u>) over to the tall slide. This was the first time your dad had ever seen you go near this particular slide (<u>voluntary</u>). At first you stood very patiently next to the slide and watched the young boy climb up the ladder and swish down the slide. Shortly thereafter you walked over to the tall ladder and slowly began to climb towards the top (<u>risk</u>). I quickly ran over to the slide when I realized that you were actually going to climb to the top of the ladder. Only being two years old, I wanted to make sure that you did not stumble or fall. I remained quietly behind the ladder as you made your way to the top. When you reached the top, you sat your small body down and waited on the landing, thinking about your next move. You had sensed the young boy's action on the slide and seemed ready to copy his feat (<u>imitation</u>). Carefully, you nudged yourself away from the landing and swished down the slippery slope. What do you think your face looked like as you gathered your thoughts at the bottom of the slide? Can you show me?*

Zoé - Was I happy?

Daddy - *Yes! Do you remember that moment? Can you show me?*

Zoé - No! (Zoe smiles and chuckles).

Daddy - *See! You do remember. As you stood on the ground near the bottom of the slide your face was filled with happiness and joy. You had* *accomplished something that you had never done before. For a brief moment you were a different person who would never be the same because a new dimension had just been added to your being (<u>pretending</u>). And this, your first journey with your new friends, the little boy and the slide, was just the beginning (<u>bonding with another human being and the environment</u>).*

Zoé - Then what did the little boy do? Tell me that part.

Daddy - *After watching your first triumph your new friend, a friendship developed without even talking, went back to the ladder and climbed to the top again (<u>alternation</u>). At the top, he turned his body over onto his stomach and swished down the slide on his tummy. Seeing this new method of going down the slide, you proceeded to climb the ladder again. I again remained behind the ladder to insure your safety. When you reached the top you, like your new friend, turned yourself over onto your tummy (<u>change</u>). This intricate position took some slick maneuvering on your part. Laying on your tummy you carefully pushed yourself away from the safety of the landing and swished down the slippery slide a second time. When you arrived at the bottom your face was once again glowing with happiness.*

Zoé - Then what did the little boy do?

Daddy - *Be patient. I'll tell you. After the tummy slide, your new friend scurried up the ladder a third time and rested on the landing. Without any talking between the two of you, you climbed the ladder and sat down behind the young boy. He waited patiently as you adjusted your legs around his body. How you knew what to do is one of the many mysteries of play. Once in place, the two of you went down the slide together. When you reached the bottom of the slide both of you were filled with a sense of delight. You smiled at each other and acknowledged your success. The young boy then ran away to another area of the park while you stood and thought about your accomplishments (<u>resolution</u>).*

Zoé - I wish I could go down a big slide like that again. Isn't there a slide like the one in Columbus in the park by Cranberry World? Maybe we can go there someday.

Daddy - *Maybe you should join the gulls and slide down that big rock. That would be fun, wouldn't it?*

Zoé - Dad, it is too cold to do that. I might be able to slide down that rock when it gets hotter outside. Oh, Dad! Look at this piece of pretty beach glass.

Daddy - *That is a jewel from the ocean. Let's run again shall we?*

Witnessing the events on that beautiful fall morning in the Park of Roses provided me with an awakening of sorts. Thanks to Zoé and the young boy I was able to make simultaneous sense out of the wonders of play. I had witnessed movement, free activity, risk, imitation, pretending, bonding, alternation, change, and resolution. Moreover, I had seen two young children who were engaged in a very <u>serious</u> activity.

Zoé's play with the young boy on the slide taught her that she could challenge herself and be triumphant. She gained an understanding of, and an adoration for, her capabilities. She also gained an appreciation and a respect for learning about, and from, other human beings and the world around her. There were no extraneous agendas or strings attached (profit or material benefits).

Since that beautiful fall morning in Columbus there have been many occasions where I have expanded my understanding of the importance of play by, *"Running with Zoé."* The wonders of play are her path to knowledge and experience about herself and her world. Like Zoé, every one of us has acquired wisdom through the wonder of play. We have created and recreated our world with play.

Games

Now that Zoé has helped introduce us to the wonder of play, let us continue in our journey towards an understanding of sport. Our next stop will be the phenomenon known as games.

Games are simply an extension of the wonders of play. To get from play to games you simply add two elements to the *Ten Wonders*. These elements are, competition and rules. Games are simply any form of playful, rule bound competition.

Simply stated, competition is our struggle for success. Human beings struggle to be successful over obstacles seen and unseen, small and large. This struggle begins with our first breath and ends when we can struggle no longer.

Competition is a construct that can often be looked upon with disdain. In America this scorn is fueled by the "Success at all costs" or "King of the hill" mentality that seems to dominate much of our lives. This brand of relentless and distasteful competition, especially when it pertains to games and sport, is often driven by greed and selfishness. Rather than focus on this, the petty end of the competitive continuum, I will try and stay focused on the humane end. In other words I will try to shed light on the positive and meaningful aspects of our competitive spirit.

The very act of women and men struggling for intimacy with another human being is a struggle for success. The challenge that women and men have in providing food and shelter for themselves and their offspring is also a struggle for success. And, a newborn baby striving to keep his or her mother's nipple in their mouth is a struggle to be successful. Games, or our playful struggle to be successful, are exercises in what it means to be alive, to be pushing forward. Competition is, and always will be, an integral part of our existence.

Games are also bound by rules, which are a prescribed guide for conduct or action. Competing individuals or teams must agree to the guidelines that will govern their conduct or action. The established guidelines govern space, time, and energy. Examples of rules governing space would be the agreed upon dimensions of a game board, size of ball, or weight of bat. Examples of rules governing time would be the length of game periods, the length of a program (figure skating and gymnastics), or the time allotted for a move in a game of chess or a serve in tennis match. Examples of rules governing energy would be the amount of force a player can exert when they check a player in ice hockey, or bump a player in soccer. In games, all individuals or groups enter the struggle for playful success voluntarily and by doing so, they agree to play according to the established rules.

Games can take many forms. They can be played between individuals, between teams of individuals, between individuals or teams and animate objects (animals), between individuals or teams and inanimate objects (not alive, i.e., sticks, balls, gloves, etc.), and between individuals or teams trying to set ideal standards or records. These five forms can occur separately or in a combination of two or more.

An example of a game between individuals would be chess where you have one human being struggling to be successful over another human being. A game between teams of individuals would be women's field hockey where you have one team of human beings struggling against another team of human beings. An example of a game between individuals or teams and an animate object would be dressage in which you have an individual or a team struggling to be successful over a horse or horses. A game between an individual or teams and an inanimate object would be golf. In golf an individual or team struggles to be successful over the inanimate clubs and the inanimate balls. Finally, an example of a game where individuals or teams are trying to set ideal standards or records would be track and field. In track and field individuals and teams struggle for faster times, longer distances, and increased heights.

As was mentioned earlier, the five game forms can occur individually or in a combination of two or more. Try, if you can, to think of a game that incorporates all five of the game forms. In other words, are there any games that incorporate individuals, teams, individuals or teams and animate objects, individuals or teams and inanimate objects, and individuals or teams trying to set ideal standards or records? Take a few moments and ponder this question.

One example of a game that satisfies all five forms is Polo. In Polo you have a playful struggle for supremacy between:

1. **Individuals** - The individual players struggle against one another,

2. **Teams** - Teams of players struggle against each other,

3. **Individuals or Teams and Animate Objects** - Individuals and teams struggle against the horse/s,

4. **Individuals or Teams and Inanimate Objects** - Individuals or teams struggle against the inanimate clubs and inanimate balls, and

5. **Individuals or Teams Trying to Set Ideal Standards or Records** - Individuals or teams try to set personal or game records.

Now it is your turn. Can you think of any other games that incorporate all five forms?

Sport

During our journey to an understanding of sport, the wonder of play became a game when we added rules and competition. A game will become sport when we add two more elements. These elements are governing bodies and physical excellence. Adding governing bodies simply means that the competitions now have persons or organizations that oversee the games. Their task is to establish and administer rules and regulations. Governing bodies must, to the best of their abilities, enforce the established rules and regulations. Enforcement is done by umpires, referees, officials, or judges.

The second element that is required in sport is physical excellence. A game becomes sport when the game is institutionalized and when the game embodies physical excellence. In other words poker is not a sport. Poker is a game. Editors who choose to place the results of a game of poker in the sport section of a newspaper are wrong.

Therefore, sport is any form of <u>playful, rule bound, competition</u> that has a <u>governing body</u> and <u>requires physical excellence</u>. Remove any one of the five components and sport is no longer sport. Take away the governing bodies and you are left with a game. Take away the physical excellence and you are left again with playful, rule bound competition, that is, Poker, Chess, Checkers, or Monopoly. Take away the rules, the struggle to be supreme, the governing bodies, and the physical prowess and what you have left is play. Sport is only sport when you have play, rules, competition, a governing body, and physical excellence. Each component is a separate and important ingredient of sport.

We now have a real, bona fide definition of sport. For many, this may be the first time that you can actually define sport. We are able to do this because we completed a journey from play - to games - to sport. Hopefully the wisdom acquired on the journey will add to your understanding of sport.

Personal Reflections on Sport

There are many rewards that human beings receive from sport. Having journeyed to a definition of sport will make it easy to discuss these rewards. When we refer to sport it is important to always remember that we are also talking about games and play. Sport is made from the sensations and elements of games and play. Sport provides a myriad of rewards to people of all ages and these rewards are fundamentally intrinsic; they make us feel good inside. Extrinsic rewards such as money, prizes, or trophies have very little to do with the intention of sport. At the deepest level the rewards from sport are sport, nothing more, nothing less. Chief among the intrinsic rewards from sport is the construct that sport is governed by rules. Sport requires all individuals or teams struggling for success to agree to established rules and to accept agreed upon disciplinary actions if the established rules are broken or disobeyed. The intention of sport is to be fair. Sport that is not fair, is not sport.

Throughout history humans have trusted reciprocal relationships to guide and serve as their moral compass. This certainty is demonstrated by the fact that in nearly every religion known to mankind there is some version of a Golden Rule, "Do Unto Others As You Would Want Others To Do Unto You." Ancient game participants learned early on that by playing fair, with both other humans and the environment, their chances for survival were greatly enhanced. Those who did not play fair were either not allowed to play or banished.

In sport, governing bodies establish and enforce the rules and regulations. An important facet of this governance is that it is done in an open and public forum. Sport is a public institution that is witnessed by millions of folks through participation, spectating, television, and radio. In today's world we do not have many institutions where the implementation and enforcement of rules and regulations is as public as the institution of sport. Unlike politics, religion, and business, sport provides an open arena where everyone can experience public fairness.

Another intrinsic reward from sport is its ability to satisfy our need to be physical. Humans are physical beings. They will always gravitate towards happenings that challenge their bodily beings. Sport has been, and always will be, a means whereby humans can experience their beings being physical.

The rewards we receive from sport also include the intrinsic rewards we receive from games. One of the many intrinsic rewards from games is that they are unbiased. In games, extraneous considerations such as gender, race, money, social status, and religion play no part in determining the outcome. The outcome of playful competition is determined by the capabilities of the individual players. As a result games can be one of the great equalizing forces of our civilization. Disparate folks can become one as they unite their individual capabilities in a common struggle for success.

In games we are often confronted with struggles that end in defeat or unfulfilled triumph. Much like a good story, it is the uncertainty of the outcome of a game that holds our attention. If we knew in advance the outcomes from our struggles, we would have little incentive to participate. Another intrinsic reward from our participation in games is that through defeat, we learn that success is not always guaranteed. Although difficult, defeat teaches us that our unfulfilled triumphs are not the end of the game or death. We learn that we can rejuvenate ourselves and struggle again and again.

Struggling for success in a game often has nothing to do with the outcome (winning). The struggle may simply be to enhance one's personal performance (to furnish completely). It is interesting to note that when children are asked to list the rewards they receive from their participation in games they, more often than not, place personal performance rewards at the top. The outcome (winning) is usually at, or near, the bottom of their list. Children's most meaningful rewards come from personal triumphs. They list things such as interacting with their friends, interacting with coaches, feeling physically fit, learning new skills and, sharing with their families, as the most important rewards. You probably have heard the statement; young children would rather play on a losing team than sit on the bench of a winning team.

The rewards we receive from sport increase dramatically when we consider play, the root of both games and sport. Play is overflowing with intrinsic rewards. Some of these rewards have already been discussed during our run with Zoé. For example, we discussed the intrinsic rewards gained from humans experiencing their bodies being physical. We also discussed the importance of bonding with other humans. Other intrinsic rewards that we receive from our participation in play, and therefore games and sport, are freedom, learning to take risks, learning through imitation, learning to bond with the environment, learning to alternate and change, and learning about resolution.

Learning about freedom (voluntary activity) is a special intrinsic reward from our participation in play. We are free to choose to play, or free to choose not to play. Our bodily beings are unconstrained. This freedom although brief, teaches humans that they can be self-governing and independent beings. When you combine this reward with the previously mentioned reward of working cooperatively with other human beings (bonding) you have the essential ingredients for an emancipated and democratic society. Play and its extensions games and sport, can be models for a free and cooperative world.

Learning to take risks is another intrinsic reward we receive from our participation in play. Risks are simply anything that frightens us. Through play we learn to take risks and in so doing we overcome our fears. Zoé's mastery of the giant slide is an excellent example of how play provides opportunities for humans to overcome their fears. Moreover, our successes in and through play inspire us to risk again. Slowly play's process of fear and mastery pushes us forward.

Still another notable reward is imitation. It is through imitation that we learn. We observe other humans and our environment and copy the movement, language, personality, and energy. We have learned what to be from copying. We have become someone or something else (pretending). Social psychologists call this phenomenon, The Social Learning Theory. At the root of this theory is the wonder of play.

Because play can be a rehearsal of things to come it is important that the imitative and pretending experiences be moral and wholesome. If human beings imitate too many immoral or unwholesome experiences, they may be rehearsing for a life filled with decadence and despair. We must realize that through play, and therefore games and sport, people are listening, people are seeing, and people are learning.

Bonding with the environment is yet another reward we receive from our participation in play. Play provides the means whereby the relationships between human beings and the environment are established. The environmental playground is our classroom. This is the arena where we learn respect and an appreciation for the world around us. Through play, games, and sport, participants learn to treasure fresh air, sparkling water, beautiful skies, and other living things. Although often overlooked, this is an extremely important reward. It provides human beings with opportunities to respect, appreciate, and therefore preserve the grandeur of our environmental playground. To create and maintain positive relationships in our environmental playground it is necessary to learn about alternation and change. Alternation and change can be two of play's finest rewards. Alternation can teach us important lessons about sharing and help us to expand our feelings towards other human beings and the environment. Alternation is facilitated by our openness to accept change. To alternate we must be willing to add to, or delete from, our thoughts, ideas, principles, habits, and customs. The wonder of play provides an infinite array of opportunities for us to learn about and practice both alternation and change.

Another reward we receive from our participation in play is that eventually it will play-out. In other words there will always be a solution or resolution. The resolutions from play could be as simple as Zoé's radiance after her success on the slide or as complex as ten judges trying to resolve the unsuccessful performance of a figure skater. The resolution could also be one of sorrow after an agonizing defeat or one of glory after an exhilarating victory. One of the great rewards from play, games, and sport is that they teach us that sooner or later, regardless of the complexity, sorrow, or glory our efforts will yield a resolution. It is our awareness of, and our anticipation for the resolution, that inspires us to play again, and again, and again.

As you have discovered, throughout history play, games, and sport have provided humans with a myriad of intrinsic rewards. These rewards have furnished the sustenance that secured our continued progress and evolution. Any phenomenon with a record of success as outstanding as sport deserves our steadfast commitment to insure continued responsible progress and honorable evolution.

Chapter V

Modern Sport - Too Far Away
A Short Story

<hr />

We must love one another or die.

- W. H. Auden

ONCE UPON A TIME IN the City of Tall Buildings a young boy was
born. His first breath and accompanying scream revealed that he was
robust and energetic. The boy's parents, hard working and respected
members of the city, were proud to share their son with relatives and
friends.

The young boy's mother dedicated herself to raising and safeguarding
the infant child and his two siblings. In her spare time she enjoyed
singing and dancing. The young boy would often imitate his mother as
she moved gracefully to the melodic rhythms of her voice. The mother
generously shared her gifts with her children.

The young boy's father worked as a Keeper of the Forests for the City
of Tall Buildings. Even before the boy could walk he would accompany
his father to work where he would observe his father caring for and
tending to the trees and wildlife. The Keeper of the Forests was an
extremely important job as the forests were integral to the survival of the

people who lived in the City of Tall Buildings. You see, the forests were home to the large elephants that provided a majority of the sustenance for the people of the city. A vibrant forest helped insure a plentiful supply of elephants.

It was during his trips to the forest with his father that the young boy began to imitate the elephant hunters who stalked their prey in late summer and early fall. From the city's most accomplished hunters the young boy learned how to run like the wind and leap like a gazelle. He learned how to fling his spear and strike his target with deadly accuracy while at the same time jumping over large rocks and bushes. Even at a very young age, the boy began to show exceptional virtuosity in the art of hunting unlike any athlete in the city. Older, accomplished hunters, eager to share their aptitudes with the young boy, would marvel at his virtuosity. People often made special trips to the forest to witness firsthand the awesome skills of the young boy.

It was customary in the City of Tall Buildings for each hunter to share the rewards from their hunt with the larger community. Every fallen elephant provided an abundance of meat, clothing, blankets and bones. No single hunter could ever consume or use all of the meat, bones, and skins that came from a single elephant. Moreover, in the City of Tall Buildings there existed an unspoken code of recipro-city. Every citizen knew that by sharing with the larger community they would somehow, someday, be reimbursed. Thus the city's best hunters knew that by sharing the rewards from their hunt they would be compensated in ways unknown to them at the moment of sharing. One example of this glorious scheme occurred when a resident of the city came to the aid of one hunter after the latter's home had been devastated by lightning. Because this particular fellow was the city's weaver of big ropes, his skills were integral to rebuilding the hunter's home. Another example occurred when a woman skilled in language and philosophy openly and freely shared her gifts with several of the hunter's children. In the City of Tall Buildings recipro-city was simply the code by which everyone lived. The community realized that their very survival depended on an unconditional sharing with, and respect for, others.

One summer, the City of Tall Buildings was struck with an immense heat wave. The Keeper of the Forest worked tirelessly trying to protect the plants and trees of the forest from the sun's scorching heat. With little water and raging temperatures, many animals that called the forest their home scattered. Sadly, many others were overcome by dehydration and died. The sweltering heat made hunting elephants almost impossible. Of the ten to twelve expert hunters in the City of Tall Buildings only one person continued to hunt, the young boy who was now nearing manhood.

Despite the hardships in the forest the young man was still successful. After each expedition he returned with an elephant. People from all over the city would await his return and, because of the scarcity of food and clothing, would offer him all sorts of goods and services in exchange for a small piece of his kill. Over time their offers increased substantially. In fact, it was absolutely astonishing to see what folks were willing to give the young man for a portion of his catch. Land barons offered pristine sections of real estate. Libation officers offered lifetime supplies of wine and spirits. Merchants and marketers offered large sailing ships filled with gold and jewels. Women and young girls offered themselves to the man in every imaginable way, each hoping to get closer, and ultimately gain from the man's success in the hunting arena. Those who had only moderate offerings, a majority of the citizens from the City of Tall Buildings, were simply left out. These folks were forced to watch from the sidelines while those with extraordinary means took their seat at the bartering banquet.

Because of his amazing skills the young man, not even twenty years of age, amassed an incredible fortune. Money, land, tall buildings, boats and ships, vehicles, food stuffs, and women were all his. Given the fortunes he gained in just one year, he realized he would never have to hunt again. Any hunting he did now would be simply to satisfy his own personal needs. Because of his enormous wealth, he cared little for the welfare of those in his family or others in his community. After all, what could they offer to a man who had everything?

Eventually the catastrophic heat began to abate. With its departure, life began to return to normal in the City of Tall Buildings. Despite having little contact with their son, the young man's father still looked after the forests while his mother enjoyed nurturing and providing for her family.

Winter was approaching and the man decided to enter the hunting arena once again. He wanted to test his skills one last time. After only forty-eight minutes of hunting, he emerged with an elephant. This particular elephant happened to be the largest he had ever fallen, a real World Champion. Hundreds of townspeople, young and old and from all walks of life, came to the edge of the forest to witness his extraordinary trophy. They watched in astonishment as he transported his kill back to his private compound. This World Champion was going to be his to keep and enjoy; he felt no need to share it with others.

The man proceeded to skin and butcher the elephant and then carefully began to stack the hundreds of pounds of meat all around him. He could barely see over the pile of ribs. There was another heap of steaks that created a wall in the shape of a half circle. Soon he was surrounded by a fortress of meat and bones. As he lay back, resting on the soft warm skins and eating large pieces of meat, he thought, "I am truly great, greater and more important than any other."

The man remained within his quarry of splendor for several days. He was absolutely consumed with himself and his abilities. He admired his trophy while at the same time engorging meat and drink. On or about the fifth day the man happened to notice a nest of small white worms peeking out from his pile of ribs. Curious, he removed a section of ribs only to find hundreds of larvae eating away at his meat. The sight of these squirming worms was almost as shocking as their stench. Frantically he began dismantling his quarry of meat and bones. Under each piece he found more and more larvae. The stink got worse and worse. Thousands of worms, now free from their host, quickly began to crawl onto the man's legs and arms. They moved up his ankles, under his pants, and began attaching themselves to the skin around his thighs and pelvis. It was not long before the larvae on his hands and arms began to hatch into flies. Looking for sustenance, the hungry newborn flies began biting his neck and behind his ears. Blood started to trickle down his shoulders. The man was slowly being enveloped by noxious sucking worms and stinging flies.

Hysterical, the man began to scream and cry out.

"Father!"

"Mother!"

"Brother!"

"Sister!"

"People of the City of Tall Buildings!"

"Please help me! Please help me!"

"Please help!"

"Help me!"

"Me!"

No one heard the man's plea for help. Not his father, mother, brother, sister, or any citizen from the City of Tall Buildings. The riotous noise from the sucking and biting insects overpowered his weakening voice.

With little breath and only a meager amount of strength remaining, the man died the next day. As the end came he was all alone, too far away. Too far away...

Chapter VI

A Conversation With Howard

Who so danceth not,
Knoweth not what cometh to pass.

Acts of John

PRIOR TO THE START OF the 1983 National Basketball Association playoffs a crew from ABC Television's *SportsBeat* with Howard Cosell, came to the Philadelphia Seventy-Sixers' pre-playoff practice site and filmed a feature story about my work as the team's Dance Conditioning Coach. For me, this was an extraordinary happening. To have an icon of sport journalism create a story about my work with this outstanding basketball team was, to say the least, unbelievable. The following conversation and fanciful sequel confirm the infinite sagacity of Howard Cosell.

From A.B.C. Television's *SportsBeat*

Howard Cosell - This is John Kilbourne who did his Master's Thesis at U.C.L.A. in "Dance And Its Relationship to Sports." He has designed a highly acclaimed exercise program based on the principles of dance. The routine only vaguely related to other fitness programs like Jackie Sorenson's aerobic dancing or the exercises of Richard Simmons. All designed to put the average body in better working order. But

John Kilbourne does not fine tune average bodies. He works with the Philadelphia Seventy-Sixers, favorites in the current N.B.A. playoffs. With players, the "Great Ones," such as the incomparable Julius Erving, Moses Malone, Andrew Toney, and Maurice Cheeks. Kilbourne has become the Seventy Sixers' thirteenth man. The twenty minutes before and the ten minutes after every Sixers' practice belong to him.

John Kilbourne - *Basically I start the practice every day. We start with this exercise program that I developed. It's about seventeen or eighteen minutes long. We go, I go through the whole body. We start with the head, we work with the hands, we warm-up all the joints, all the muscles of the body, take them (the players) through a very good stretching program, before every practice. You've got to warm-up your body before you start. You just can't put your tennis shoes on and start dunking.*

Howard - The Sixers are the only N.B.A. team employing a full-time strength and flexibility instructor. Sixer coach Billy Cunningham believes he can reduce injuries this way. Kilbourne frequently compares athletes to race horses, big investments needing constant special care. The strongest supporter of Kilbourne's work is a thoroughbred and a ballerina, the "Doctor," Julius Erving.

John - *Julius is a virtuoso basketball player. In dance you have your virtuosos. He is such a beautiful athlete. He has told me that this year he feels very good for this late into the season because of these exercises. In terms of Julius, it will just maybe help him play another couple of years. There's no reason an athlete should only play basketball four or five years if they take care of themselves. Julius takes care of himself.*

Julius Erving - If John's program has enhanced and increased my flexibility then I think it also puts my mind a little more at ease and makes me more comfortable with the things that I attempt to do on the court.

Howard - Kilbourne admits that much of his work is a mental game. The Sixers, a team under immense pressure. A team where in any result, less than an N.B.A. title would constitute a losing season. The music playing over the exercises serves to flush out such draining distractions.

Andrew Toney - I think the music is good because some days you might be feeling low or down, or feeling tired and you don't feel like stretching. And then once you hear a different type of sound, you tend to get your intensity back into it, you tend to concentrate a little more, and then you tend to stretch more.

Julius - We all line up on the floor and he turns the music on. It brings about a oneness. It sort of eliminates a lot of the thoughts and a lot of the distractions that are naturally around. And I guess if you want to talk about pressure, pressure could be one of those distractions.

John - This game is so intense. You can get the players into a good mood, singing, snapping their fingers, laughing, being happy. If you're happy, you're going to win. I've seen so many teams and when you watch them play, they're not happy. If you're happy, you're into a rhythm, you're flowing. This team is very happy...

Personal Reflections

To me, there have always been things enigmatic about sport, things that were tremendously exciting, but things that I could never figure out. I am sure that many of you have been intrigued by these same mysteries. It was after my tenure with the Philadelphia Seventy-Sixers that I began to fully realize the artistry inherent in sport. Sport fulfills two essential aesthetic cravings. One craving is the need we all have to express ourselves. A second craving is our need to experience human beauty. Sport turns people on because it provides opportunities for human beings to experience and witness expressive beauty. Sport is "The People's Art."

To help you understand the notion of sport as a form of artistic expression, I am going to ask you to pretend. I am going to ask you to pretend that Howard Cosell has returned to do a sequel to our previous conversation. I have often fantasized about just such a conversation. What would I like Mr. Cosell to examine now that I have had time to reflect on our earlier conversation?

To help bring Howard (and other departed beings who you may wish to visit with) back, I suggest we use the following poem. It was given to me when my own father passed on. I often use this poem to open-up dialogue between myself and departed relatives and mentors. You may wish to do the same.

Do not stand at my grave and weep,

I am not there I do not sleep.

I am a thousand winds that blow,

I am the diamond glints on snow.

I am the sunshine on ripened grain,

I am the gentle autumn rain.

When you awaken in the morning's hush,

I am the swift uplifting rush of quiet birds in circled flight.

I am the soft stars that shine at night.

Do not stand at my grave and cry,

I am not there, I did not die.

- Author Unknown

A Fanciful Sequel To:
A Conversation With Howard

Howard Cosell *(*In the After-Life*)* - John Kilbourne, or shall I call you Dr. Kilbourne? Since we last talked you completed your doctorate at The Ohio State University in Sport Studies, specifically Sport Philosophy. Is this true? Congratulations!

John Kilbourne – Yes, thank you for the kind words. John will be fine.

Howard - When we last met you and the Sixers' Team were on your way to the National Basketball Association playoffs. We all know that the 1983 Philadelphia Seventy-Sixers eventually won the Championship in near ideal form. We also know that the team had an extraordinary year in terms of player games lost due to injury. In addition to the physical aspects, flexibility, balance, coordination and preventing injuries, what else did your dance exercise program do for this team?

John - If you asked me this question when we met last, I would not have been able to discuss all of the benefits that came from the dance program. At that point I simply was not aware of them. It was actually listening to the players' remarks during your interview in 1983 that started me thinking about other contributions. Now, after working with hundreds of athletes over a period of nearly twenty-five years, I can clearly recognize the many benefits that come from the application of dance to sport.

First, the time we had together at the start of each practice session was the only time that every member of the team was doing the same exact thing at the same exact time. For approximately thirty minutes there was mental and physical unity. Each player, whether they be the superstar or the twelfth player off the bench, came together and moved together as one. As Julius said, the exercises brought about a "oneness." For this team, or any team for that matter, coming together as a team is essential for success. For example, at the start of the 1982-83 Sixers' season there was tremendous concern about the ability of Julius Erving and Moses Malone to come together and share the limelight and glory. I think the camaraderie that unfolded at the start of every practice helped, not only Julius and Moses, but every player adjust to each other. Moreover, this wholeness seemed to carry over into practice and games.

Howard - Wasn't it somewhat of a risk for these inimitable basketball players to be performing these peculiar dance exercises in public? Didn't they feel somewhat embarrassed?

John - *It is interesting that you ask this. Taking a risk was actually another advantage the players gained from doing these exercises. Before I explain, let me tell you that over the years I have probably been asked this question more often than any other. Believe me, it has not been easy to convince every athlete that I have worked with, that dance can be beneficial to their athletic performance. I remember once being asked by a hesitant athlete if these exercises would prevent him from having children. He thought that by somehow increasing his flexibility he would damage his body parts that are necessary for conceiving a child.*

What was exciting about the dance program with the Seventy-Sixers was that every player was taking a risk together. No player was exempt from exposing themselves to each other and to the world around them. For some, this was quite a stretch (literally and figuratively). It was the organic interrelatedness of the players during the exercise program that enabled many of them to master their fear of doing something out-of-the-ordinary.

This communal risk taking and mastery was a tremendous asset in the team's quest for excellence.

Howard - Speaking of excellence. You happened to have worked with one of basketball's greatest players, the virtuoso Julius "Dr. J" Erving. I think I referred to Julius as a "Ballerina." What did Julius mean to the success of your program?

John - *Well, first of all I need to correct you on the use of the word "Ballerina." The proper term would be "Ballerino." Ballerinas are women. Frankly, without Julius there would have been no program with the Seventy-Sixers. It was because Julius felt that the dance program was important that I was hired. Julius has tremendous insight. Furthermore, my two years with Julius taught me more about sport than any person I have come in contact with during my life in and through sport. One of his greatest lessons came from witnessing the brilliance of his bodily being. His effulgence convinced me that sport, like dance, was a form of artistic expression. One of the reasons Julius was so convincing was that he was able to use his body to create new and extraordinary ways to play the game of basketball. He was a sport artist. Human movement and creativity just happen to be two of the connectors that couple sport to art.*

Ever since the beginning of time human beings have been fascinated by the natural beauty of the human body. When juxtaposed against its surroundings the human body is atypical, it stands apart from nature and other living things. It is our awareness of this detachment that creates our fascination with the body, and thus our sense of beauty. The arena of sport has always been a gallery for the expression of the unique, natural beauty of the human being. Fortunately I was able to share in the glorious expression of one of the great, unique, natural, sport artists of all time, "Dr. J."

Julius' ability to invent new ways of achieving success on the basketball court is another reason that his play can be considered a form of artistic expression. This ability is what artists call creativity.

Creativity is an important aspect of sport. I define creativity as: <u>The emergence as a result of intense action of a new product or order based on the willingness of an individual or team to take risks and to embrace their individuality and the environment.</u> In order for something to be creative it first of all must <u>emerge</u> or be born. I could have had the idea of applying dance conditioning to sport in my mind my entire life. It became creative when it emerged or was born. Moreover, creativity is a result of <u>intense action</u>. People have often remarked how fortunate I was to have been hired by the Seventy-Sixers and to have been part of a team that won a World Championship. What many of these folks do not understand is that it took a lot of effort (<u>intense action</u>) to make this happen. For example, during my tenure with Coach Brown at UCLA, I would drive all over Los Angeles during the summer months and give away free samples of my conditioning program to teams participating in the National Basketball Association Summer Pro-league. It was the willingness of some of the coaches and players participating in the Summer League to take <u>risks</u> and allow me to share my unique dance conditioning talents (<u>a new order - individuality</u>) in their <u>environment</u> (basketball) that eventually led to me being hired as the first full-time conditioning coach in the NBA.

Because sport is governed by rules, coaches and players must utilize their creativity to gain a fair advantage. In other words, success can be enhanced by using creative techniques and strategies within the confines of the rules. Candy Cummings and the curve ball in baseball, Dean Smith and the four corners offense in basketball, Jane Torvill and Christopher Dean in ice dancing, Dick Fosbury in the high jump, Nadia Comaneci in gymnastics, and of course Julius "Dr. J" Erving in basketball, are just some examples of sport participants who have enhanced personal and team performance using their creativity.

Howard - So you're telling me that one of the great lessons you received from "Dr. J" was that he shared with you the artistry of sport.

You realize John, that there are many people who do not share your feelings about sport being a form of art? I, having spent many years as a friend of, and reporting on Muhammad Ali, happen to share your sentiment that sport is a form of art and athletes are artists. Ali was a master of artistic expression. To persuade the naysayers, what else could you share about your work that would help them understand sport as a form of art?

John - Well, in addition to the camaraderie, the risk, the human body, and creativity, sport and art share a root that is made from play and competition. All of the sensations that go into making play are involved in the constitution and character of both sport and art. In addition, there is competition in all forms of sport as well as art. Artists continually struggle to be successful over their mediums, that is, their physical bodies if they dance, sing, or act, their clay if they sculpt, their canvas and pallet if they paint. Because of these tight bonds, you simply cannot separate art from sport.

Howard - You mentioned earlier about the natural beauty of sport. Are you inferring that sport also has aesthetic qualities?

John - Most definitely. If you look back in history you will see that the Ancient Greeks defined aesthetic (aisthetikos) simply as, "to perceive beauty." I think their definition is a good one. After all, the Ancient Greeks were known for their artistic excellence. Unfortunately, what has hurt the debate about sport being a form of artistic expression is that the notion of what is aesthetic or artistic has become far too academic. Who am I to suggest what others should consider beautiful? I often tell the students in my college classes that what may be beautiful to one student may be offensive to another. Beauty, and therefore art, are very personal. It depends upon your personal, "life suitcase."

When you ask elite athletes, both amateur and professional, if they consider their sport a form of art, many answer yes. Believe me, I have asked this question many times and the answers are often yes. Sport, for many folks is pleasing to their senses and therefore aesthetic. It makes them happy. No one has any right to deny them these delightful sensations.

Howard - "It makes them happy." It's funny that you would say that. You said that in our original interview as well. Just what do you mean by, "It makes them happy?"

John - *Mr. Cosell, I have to tell you that I have watched our earlier interview numerous times and shown it during many classes and lectures and each time I hear myself say, "You can get the players into a good mood, singing, snapping their fingers, laughing, being happy," I start laughing myself. I have often said to myself, "Now that was a silly statement." However, the more I thought about that statement, the more I realized that being blissful isn't so ridiculous after all. Moving and singing (I don't think Bobby Jones sang much) to the taped music of Luther Vandross and others created honest and festive happiness. Luther Vandross says it best with his song, "Having A Party." This song was often used to accompany the dance exercises.*

> *Roll back the rug everybody, move all the tables and chairs.*
> *We're going to have a good time tonight.*
> *Every time that we meet, we skip and we dip to the beat.*
> *What in the world could be better than getting together.*
> *- Luther Vandross*

John - *Dancing and singing together helped to create a happy team. If you're happy, you are a winner. I think I said that as well. If you're happy, you're into a rhythm, you're flowing with yourself and with the world around you. You become an artist in that it is **you**, that you are creating and expressing. This is the beauty of sport.*

Howard – Yes indeed John. It seems you have been thinking a lot about human nature and sport since our last meeting. Excellent work. I see that my time here is about up. I must return to my *Angelic* responsibilities. I want to thank you for giving me this opportunity to live again through your world of sport and art. I thoroughly enjoyed our time together. Please bring me back any time. You can rest assured that I am not sleeping.

John - Mr. Cosell, it is you whom I should be thanking. I cannot tell you what a pleasure it was to be present with you again. Your insight continues to help me understand sport. Today's visit was no different. Oh, before you leave. If you see them, please give my regards to my father Charles, my sister Janett, my wife's father Darwin, A. Bartlett Giamatti, and Arthur Ashe. Tell them that through the dance of life I am really trying to enlighten the world of sport.

Chapter VII

Dance for Athletes

━━◆◇◆━━

Winning in a Waltz and Pirouette

It may not have been a coincidence that the Philadelphia 76ers danced into the NBA playoffs with a 65-17 regular-season record. The Sixers, after all, have used a ballet instructor named John Kilbourne throughout the season as a flexibility and coordination coach. Kilbourne did graduate work at UCLA under the noted prima ballerina Mia Slavenska and, while there, helped condition the 1979-80 Bruin team that went to the NCAA Final Four. He later conducted clinics for the Portland Trail Blazers and Phoenix Suns and moved to Philadelphia last September to work with the 76ers. He also teaches part time at the Philadelphia College of the Performing Arts.

Kilbourne conducts workouts before every Sixer practice and overseas stretching routines on game days. The purpose of the workouts, which last 20 minutes and include dance moves to music by Aretha Franklin, among others, is to help the players become more limber, jump higher and avoid injury. By having the players move together rhythmically, Kilbourne also believes he helps them "concentrate as a team." Philly Coach Billy Cunningham is all for the ballet instructions. "What sold me is the way the players responded and did the exercises," he says. "In the past we did some flexibility training, but a player always led. With supervision it's much better." All of which is vindication of sorts for Kilbourne who took up dance only after being cut from his high school basketball team.

- Jerry Kirshenbaum, Sports Illustrated

Most professional basketball players can't hit major league pitching, finish a marathon, pole vault as high as a basket or return a Roscoe Tanner serve. But as a group, in the view of a majority of experts polled by the Los Angeles Times, they are the best athletes playing any sport today.

- Bill Shirley

THE EXPERTS WHO SELECTED PROFESSIONAL basketball players as the best athletes playing any sport today evaluated the athletes in terms of physical strength, skill, endurance, durability, flexibility, agility, quickness, reflexes, grace and eye-hand coordination. Professional basketball players, most of the experts said best exemplify these qualities.

The dance conditioning exercises that I developed for basketball players were a supplement to basketball practice. The exercises were designed to enhance speed, durability, flexibility, agility, quickness, reflexes, grace and strength in addition to reducing basketball related injuries.

To achieve excellence in conditioning one must train the mental as well as the physical. The mind/body relationship is the foundation of "complete" conditioning. Included in *Running With Zoé* is information on and about the dance conditioning for athletes program I developed. The information included is from a book I wrote during my tenure with the Philadelphia Seventy-Sixers (1982-84). Based on current conditioning research and practice, I have added additional information where appropriate.

Principals of Conditioning

In evaluating individual and team conditioning it is important to do so in terms of the five basic principles of conditioning. If as an athlete or coach you are meeting their criteria you can rest assured that your team and or individual success will be at a maximum.

Specificity

The specificity principle states that the results of conditioning are specific to the activities performed. More simply stated specificity means that conditioning exercises, drills and skill practice should be directly related to the game, sport, or movement activity (dance) (Stigleman, p. 19). As applied to basketball specificity means that quality basketball requires practicing, conditioning for, and studying the skills important to basketball.

Overloading

The overload principle states that the intensity of exercise must be fairly great in relation to a person's existing state of fitness and must be steadily increased in order to produce an improvement in physical capacity. In general, overloading means doing more, faster, longer, higher, more often (Stigleman, p. 22).

Individuality

Individuality simply means that different individuals have unique responses to different exercises. For this reason conditioning programs should take into account the physical and psychological uniqueness of each individual (Stigleman, p. 23).

Maintenance

Once a desired level of conditioning has been attained by the use of overloading it must be maintained or the body deconditions; the principle of maintenance is "use it or lose it" (Stigleman, p. 25). An athlete must continually work to maintain his/her existing state of fitness. It doesn't take long to lose the quality conditioning you achieve during the basketball season. As an athlete grows older it becomes more difficult to recondition the physical body in preparation for the next season. Maintenance is key to a long and prosperous career in professional basketball.

Motivation

An indifferent attitude, or one of mechanically plodding along the line of least resistance on the chance that something may happen, will not bring perfection. The success of any act, no matter how simple or complex, depends upon a conscious direction of efforts towards the ideal (H'Doubler). Motivation is a key component of conditioning. As John Wooden, the legendary U.C.L.A. basketball coach says, "Success is the peace of mind which is a direct result of self-satisfaction in knowing you did your best to become the best that you are capable of becoming. (Wooden).

Flexibility, Rhythm, Coordination, Relaxation, Isolation, Music, Balance

The exercising as a group puts us on the same wavelength simultaneously. That's very helpful to the coaching staff. We usually go from stretching right into a warm-up exercise we call our sideline break. Rather than doing individual stretches without the music and without John, which would probably have guys going into that sideline break at different paces, this takes us into it all at the same time (Julius "Dr. J" Erving).

During my tenure as head basketball coach at U.C.L.A., John Kilbourne developed an off-season and pre-practice conditioning program for the U.C.L.A. team. It provided the players an opportunity to develop flexibility, rhythm and coordination and balance while greatly reducing injuries (Larry Brown).

Flexibility

I've always been a proponent of stretching and flexibility. I think it's more important than how strength is usually perceived. People think of strength in terms of bulk and I see strength as being more coordination and flexibility. Having bulk doesn't make a big difference in professional basketball. A guy 210 can move a guy 250 out of the lane if he knows how to align himself and has the flexibility to put himself in that type of position (Erving).

Flexibility is the range of motion in a joint or a combination of joints. Lack of flexibility is one of the most frequent causes of improper or poor movement. Lack of flexibility may also contribute to many athletic injuries (Swanbom). With poor flexibility, speed and efficiency is hindered since the muscles have to work harder to bring about maximum length. Extra work results in a greater loss of energy and will hinder the athletic performance. By increasing flexibility of the ankles, legs, hips and trunk greater speed can be achieved and energy conserved allowing an athlete to run faster and jump higher (Swanbom).

Flexibility training is the least researched and least understood component of physical conditioning. It has been seriously overlooked as an important aspect of physical conditioning. Donald L. Cooper, MD, says, "Strength, endurance, agility and explosive power are the qualities most coaches want for their athletes. But flexibility, which often is overlooked in a well-conditioned athlete, can enhance all the other desirable attributes and help prevent injuries" (Cooper, p. 114).

John Jesse, RPT, decried what he found to be, "An overemphasis on strength training at the expense of flexibility and specificity for the sport at hand" (Schultz, p. 109).

In the early 1940's Thomas Cureton, Ph.D. proposed that, "Flexibility exercises may be given for conditioning in the sense that full range contraction and extension… is excellent massage and exercise for the muscles, producing both a physical elongation and a strengthening of the musculature." Such exercises, he added, "if built up a to a sufficient dosage may condition muscles, tendons, ligaments, and bones to a greater tensile strength and elasticity, a factor which is basic to preventing injuries in many sports" (Cureton, p. 381).

Almost twenty years later another pioneer in flexibility research, Dr. Herbert A. DeVries, found that "Under certain conditions, the use of static stretching technique following unaccustomed exercise seems to provide some measure of prevention of ensuing muscular distress and that static stretching seems to provide a useful technique for the relief of chronic muscular distress such as shin splints in some athletes" (DeVries, p. 479).

The above mentioned research of Dr. Herbert A. DeVries is very important and should not be overlooked. It is important for athletes to take ten to fifteen minutes following their practices and games to stretch out and warm-down. When you invest time and energy in your conditioning program it is important to complete it with a thorough warm-down. This will enable the body to recover and will relieve soreness in muscles and joints.

A good example of the warm-down principle is its application with thoroughbred race horses. Seldom do professional horse trainers take their champion horses and put them back into the stalls immediately following a race. They spend considerable time warming them down to insure quality conditioning with minimum soreness and maximum output. This same philosophy should be applied to athletic conditioning.

A more contemporary pioneer in flexibility research is Jean Couch, author of The Runner's World Yoga Book. She says, "By stretching the areas that have been contracting you can reduce the amount of tension built up in the muscular system. If you don't stretch, tightness will increase and make muscles hard, non-resilient and more susceptible to injury" (Counch, p. 84).

Development

Flexibility is developed by "stretching," or slowly increasing the range of motion through which the joint is moved. The overload principle as applied to flexibility means attempting to progressively increase the range of motion through which one attempts to move (Stigleman, p. 61). When stretching the athlete must also utilize the maintenance principle of conditioning to insure continued flexibility.

Player-coach Tom McGraw of the Cleveland Indians baseball team says, "It's a matter of conditioning the body to stretch as much as possible; muscle flexibility is the key to stopping injuries (O'Sullivan, p. 109)."

The development of an athlete's flexibility must be a part of every conditioning program, Donald Cooper, MD, insists, "Stretching exercises need to be brought out from under the piles of weight-lifting machine literature; properly taught and put back into every athlete's year-round program. The wise coach will have his athletes use their flexibility program and stretch properly before practice. This should be done to avoid muscle strains and to maintain and increase the athlete's flexibility. Increasing the range of motion at the joints tends to reduce the frequency of injury. We believe that the flexible athlete performs better and is less likely to be injured (Cooper, p. 114)."

Flexibility Defined

There are three kinds of stretching: Static, ballistic and reciprocal. Static, or slow, gradual, passive stretching is defined as the method involving a held position of greatest possible length (DeVries, p.

223). Ballistic, or bobbing, bouncing, jerking stretching is defined as the method involving movements characterized by jerks and pulls upon the body segments to be stretched (DeVries, p. 223). Reciprocal stretching is based on, "The psychological premise that contraction of a muscle is followed by lengthening relaxation, and/or inhibition of the antagonistic muscles (Klafs)."

The *Dance for Athletes* conditioning program utilizes a combination of ballistic and static exercises often utilizing the reciprocal technique. A combination such as this is the most thorough way to condition athletes in flexibility training. With the use of ballistic stretching the athlete will produce a mild sweat, provide circulatory warm-up and be somewhat challenged and excited. Fred Kasch, PhD, Professor of exercise physiology at San Diego State University agrees, "I think we may have overdone static work at the expense of ballistic exercise. I favor a blend of both. For one thing static stretching is boring. Ballistic exercises make sense because so many athletic activities are ballistic in nature (Schultz, p. 109)."

Another important characteristic of the ballistic program is the lubrication of the joint capsule. With the use of moderate ballistic exercises the fluid which surrounds the joints of the body is sufficiently warmed up allowing freer flow of nerves and blood. The same principles can be applied to properly warmed-up muscle. By warming up the body prior to an athletic event with moderate ballistic exercises you loosen the musculature and allow for smooth and free passage for nerves and blood. This is a very important aspect of ballistic type flexibility exercises.

Current Research (2008) - "Stretching The Truth" by Gretchen Reynolds

WHEN DUANE KNUDSON, a professor of kinesiology at California State University, Chico, looks around campus at athletes warming up before practice, he sees one dangerous mistake after another. "They're stretching, touching their toes. . . ." He sighs. "It's discouraging." If you're like most of us, you were taught the importance of warm-up exercises back in grade school, and you've likely continued with pretty much the same routine ever since. Science, however, has moved on. Researchers now believe that some of the more entrenched elements of many athletes' warm-up regimens are not only a waste of time but actually bad for you. The old presumption that holding a stretch for 20 to 30 seconds — known as static stretching — primes muscles for a workout is dead wrong. It actually weakens them. In a recent study conducted at the University of Nevada, Las Vegas, athletes generated less force from their leg muscles after static stretching than they did after not stretching at all. Other studies have found that this stretching decreases muscle strength by as much as 30 percent. Also, stretching one leg's muscles can reduce strength in the other leg as well, probably because the central nervous system rebels against the movements. "There is a neuromuscular inhibitory response to static stretching," says Malachy McHugh, the director of research at the Nicholas Institute of Sports Medicine and Athletic Trauma at Lenox Hill Hospital in New York City. The straining muscle becomes less responsive and stays weakened for up to 30 minutes after stretching, which is not how an athlete wants to begin a workout. THE RIGHT WARM-UP should do two things: loosen muscles and tendons to increase the range of motion of various joints, and literally warm up the body. When you're at rest, there's less blood flow to muscles and tendons, and they stiffen. "You need to make tissues and tendons compliant before beginning exercise," Knudson says. A well-designed warm-up starts by increasing body heat and blood flow. Warm muscles and dilated blood vessels pull oxygen from the bloodstream more efficiently and use stored muscle fuel more effectively (Reynolds).

Rhythm, Coordination, Relaxation, Isolation

The entire pre-practice conditioning program is coordinated rhythmically to music.

The musical accompaniment provides an efficient time keeping mechanism. The time in seconds of each exercise is very important and the musical accompaniment provides an exciting and accurate time keeping system for the conditioning program.

"Because strength is easier to develop than other qualities, athletes have spent more time improving strength rather than developing speed, timing, balance and other skills that would put their strength to greater use in performance. Who can bench press the most? Who can squat with the greatest weight? Who cares? What good is it on the football field or the track? (Jesse, p. 46)." The above quote is from John P. Jesse, RPT. Mr. Jesse is a physical fitness consultant to many professional athletes. Conditioning for strength alone does not complete overall movement development. Athletes can enhance their performance by putting their strength to efficient use with the development of muscular rhythm, coordination and balance.

To the ancient Greeks whose art works are exquisite studies in rhythm, the word rhythm meant, "flow or measured flow (Miller, p. 24)." That is also its meaning today: "harmonious and regular recurrence of motion or sound (Miller, p. 24)."

William H. "Little Bill" Miller, a leading proponent of rhythm in movement provides an excellent introduction to rhythm and coordination in his book: How to Relax; Scientific Body Control.

> In the human body the flow of the involuntary muscles is a beautiful balance of poise and rhythm. The beat of the heart, its contraction, its pause, its relaxing, is rhythmic; the measured expansion and contraction of the chest in breathing is rhythmic. There is response to rhythmic sound, such as the tick of a clock, the steady drip of water. It is the muscles under our control which must be so relaxed and conditioned that they will flow in harmony with the body's involuntary rhythm. It is impossible for us to produce rhythmic actions deliberately. Only when a movement is repeated until it is performed with no conscious thought, no deliberate effort, is there natural rhythm. The rhythmic harmony of the muscular system - in other words, perfect body flow - permits freer circulation of the blood, which in turn tones up the body. And in the graceful movements resulting from the rhythmic balance, there is a saving of energy, and consequently less fatigue and greater endurance (Miller, 1945, p. 24-25).

Martha Graham, the famous American Modern Dancer, believed that movement flow (rhythm) was a result of coordination. She described coordination in dance as, "Unity of body produced by emotional physical balance. In technique, it (coordination) means so to train all elements of the body - legs, arms, torso, etc. - as to make them equally important and equally efficient. It means a state of relativity of members in use that results in flow of movement (Graham p. 133-143)." For an athlete to develop rhythm or flow of movement, coordination exercises must be introduced into their conditioning vocabulary. Two conditioning concepts are necessary for this development. These are differential relaxation and isolation. Differential relaxation is a conditioning concept developed by Edmund Jacobson. It refers to relaxation of unnecessary muscle tension during movement (Jacobson). Differential relaxation involves decreasing unnecessary tension while maintaining the proper muscle action necessary for the movement being performed. This will allow for more harmonious movement flow with minimum energy loss.

Athletes often display excess muscle tension throughout their bodies. Relaxing unnecessary tension and concentrating on the areas that you wish to strengthen, etc. increases the efficiency of the body and allows for a more coherent flow of movement. Differential relaxation is an important element of conditioning. In addition excess muscle tension requires a continuous supply of energy and can contribute to fatigue.

Isolation is an extension of differential relaxation. It refers to the ability to command movement in one area of the body while maintaining other areas. For example, basketball players can learn that they can move their torsos laterally from side to side while maintaining stationary in the lower body. Isolation requires a high level of awareness of specific body parts and the ability to coordinate those parts against other body parts. The dance warm-up exercises are designed to develop differential relaxation and isolation. Through the application of these conditioning techniques basketball players can develop rhythmic harmony in their movement vocabulary. And with the rhythmic harmony there is a saving of energy, and consequently less fatigue and greater endurance.

There are many advantages to teaching differential relaxation and isolation to basketball players. For example, a basketball player who has the ability to isolate his torso while maintaining a stationary lower body can weave his way through opposition and increase his potential in both scoring and rebounding. A basketball player who practices these techniques will exhibit less tension while playing and have an expanded movement vocabulary.

To develop rhythm and coordination differential relaxation and isolation must be practiced.

Rhythm and Music

John brings the music in, which I think helps everyone's concentration to get right into it at the same time, start and finish at the same time. And he has taken some of the things we were already doing as a team a step further, defined it into what has been his life's work and then shared it with us (Erving).

I think the music is good because some days you might be feeling low or down or tired and you don't feel like stretching and then once you hear a different type of sound you tend to get your intensity back into it and concentrate a little more and then you tend to stretch a little more (Andrew Toney).

The pre-practice program was an exciting and interesting approach to starting practice. The use of music kept all of the players working together and provided for added concentration during the exercises (Larry Brown).

"The rhythm that is to turn every movement into gesture, and the dancer (basketball player) himself into a creature liberated from the usual bonds of gravitational and muscular inertia, is most readily established by music (Langer, p. 203)." This quote is from Susanne Langer a noted philosopher in the arts. It points out the importance of using music in the development of rhythm. Using music to enhance harmonious and measured flow (rhythm) is an integral component of the dance warm-up program.

Using music as accompaniment while conditioning has many advantages. Jacques Dalcroze, the well known Swiss music-dance movement therapist of the early 1900's says, "The rhythm in hearing or in creating harmonies is not separate from, but rather intimately linked to, rhythm in seeing and moving (Kirstein, p. 286)." By using musical accompaniment with movement in conditioning the basketball player like the dancer can enhance the expression produced by the central nervous system and amplify or narrow his results to their desired need. Martha Graham says, "Primarily it is the nervous system that is the instrument of expression. This is the reason music, with its sound and rhythm, is universally the great moving force of the world. It affects animals as well as human beings (Graham, p. 45-46)."

The use of music in athletic conditioning to develop harmonious and measured flow (rhythm) is not totally new. There are recorded instances where coaches have improved their athletes through the use of musical accompaniment. One such instance was prior to World War II when Boyd Comstock the well known track coach of the University of Southern California was engaged by Mussolini to work with Italian athletes in preparation for the Olympic Games. Coach Comstock worked tirelessly at the task and it seemed almost hopeless until the clever American trainer hit on an idea. He had observed that the Italian athletes were fond of music. "Could the natural rhythm and coordination they showed in singing be applied to their conditioning in track? He had his track athletes sing as they ran, jumped and hurdled. Almost miraculous improvement resulted in their performances from this use of music in the athletes' conditioning (Miller, p. 26-7)."

Another advantage of using music in conditioning is the effect it has on the athletes' attitudes toward practice and competition. Many professional athletes use music prior to their athletic event as a form of relaxation. This helps to free their minds and bodies of unnecessary tensions. Magic Johnson of the Los Angeles Lakers Basketball team talks about this application of music to his pre-game conditioning. "Hopped in my bed, told the operator to hold the calls, took my box (cassette recorder) turned on my tunes and jammed (relaxed) (Papanek)."

Larry Brown, the former U.C.L.A. head coach, spoke most favorably of the use of music prior to practices at U.C.L.A. "With all the worries these kids have: school, studies, girls, cars, etc. the music gets their heads together quickly (Brown)." Coach Brown was speaking of the importance of music in relaxing and isolating the players prior to practice.

Still another example of this application in the use of music was following the U.C.L.A. Basketball team's loss to the University of Southern California at the Sports Arena in 1979-80. The following days practice was crowded with eager newspaper writers and television reporters. The players were somewhat embarrassed by their loss to the U.S.C. Trojans. As soon as the pre-practice conditioning program started and the music was turned on, the players began singing along and snapping their fingers to the familiar rhythms of the music. Unconsciously they were relaxing and isolating themselves in preparation for practice. It was not long before the embarrassment of the loss was forgotten and practice was operating again as usual.

The use of music (rhythm, measured flow) in conditioning will also enable the athlete to measure in time the length or period of his exercises. The skilled dancer uses music as a method of keeping time as he goes through his conditioning regime. The rhythm of the music will help keep the entire team together as they practice their warm-up exercises. It also enables the athletes to practice certain static stretching exercises for a prescribed length of time using the number of beats per measure as the time keeping device.

The use of music is a very important aspect in the training of basketball players. Its application to the training of athletes is still in the formative stages. The effect music can have on the harmonious flow of an athlete's movement and the effect it can have on the emotional outlook (relaxation) of an athlete are worthwhile areas of exploration and suggest for music's continued use in athletic conditioning.

Balance

Balance is yet another important concept in the training of skilled basketball players. The late Ida Rolf, a leading proponent of balance in the human body says, "Balance in the body does not reveal itself to the dilettante, it is a matter of intuition, experience, knowledge and study (Rolf, Ida, p. 12)."

"Balance reveals the flow of gravitational energy through the body (Rolf, Ida, p. 30)."

Gravity is an enemy to a body without balance and symmetry and is a friend to a well balanced body. A balanced body is less subject to the forces of gravity. By aligning the body and developing the symmetry of the structure, the body can operate more efficiently with less likelihood of injury and greater endurance. Again Ida Rolf says, "A Body whose components are symmetrically distributed around a vertical line dissipates less of its energy in meaningless tension (Rolf, p. 204)."

The concepts of alignment, centering and symmetry, all necessary for balance in the human body, are important components of the pre-practice, post-practice and strengthening exercises. Exercises that incorporate these concepts should be an integral part of a skilled basketball player's vocabulary. Their use in the training of basketball players is seriously overlooked. Many injuries could be prevented and performances enhanced through the application of balance, alignment, symmetry and centering, to athletic conditioning.

In order to develop balance the athlete must take the time needed to develop correct posture. Posture (the position or carriage of the body in standing or sitting) is critical in the development of efficiency in athletics. The vertical line of the body must be maintained while the components of the body are symmetrically distributed around this axis.

Running, Endurance

Successful basketball in the 1980's will be a running game. The players and teams that enjoy success will run.

There are three areas of training that need to be developed in terms of running. These three areas are running skill, running flexibility and running endurance. Running skill can best be developed by running. Herschel Walker, one of the greatest runners of all time, learned to run simply by running. He ran forwards, backwards and from side to side. He ran up hills, down hills, slow, fast and often. When he ran on the track he often would pull a tire loaded with stones attached to his waist with a long rope. This increased his leg strength and the strength of the deep intrinsic muscles of his pelvis.

It is important to make your running training applicable to the sport of basketball.

In other words try to run on the court with proper clothing and shoes (specificity). Push yourself at all times. Always run back defensively. When given the opportunity run the ball up the court and to the basket with speed, skill and power.

Running skill can also be enhanced by running backwards. Basketball is a game of movement in all directions and running backwards will provide increased strength in the hamstring muscles and deep intrinsic muscles of the pelvis. Maurice Cheeks the Philadelphia Seventy-Sixers' All-Star guard can run backwards with almost the same efficiency that he runs forwards. This is a tremendous asset to his fast break and to his superb defensive skills.Running flexibility is a key component to efficient running. By increasing the flexibility of the ankles, legs, hips and trunk greater speed can be achieved and energy conserved allowing an athlete to run faster and jump higher.

When developing running endurance it is important to realize that everyone has a certain limit to which his or her heart and circulation system is able to provide oxygen to the working tissues (Individuality). This limit is called maximum aerobic capacity. To develop endurance one does not need to work at maximum aerobic capacity. A good measure of cardiovascular fitness or endurance can be achieved by working at exercise intensity between 60 and 80 percent of your maximum aerobic capacity.

One suggested method of determining your individual exercise intensity is to calculate your maximum heart rate and then try to exercise at between 60 and 80 percent of this maximum. Your maximum heart rate can be estimated by subtracting your age from 220. For example maximum heart rate for a 22 year old would be 198 heart beats per minute. You can estimate your heart rate during exercise by counting your heart rate (pulse) for 10 seconds immediately following exercise and then multiplying by six to obtain a count for one minute. You should try to reach a level that is between 60 and 80 percent of your maximum rate. For example a 22 year old should exercise at levels of heart rate between 120 and 160 heart beats per minute.

When you run to increase your running skill and endurance it is important to do so in the context of the game of basketball. Catch long passes while running at top speed. Chase opposing players on defense to test your speed. Bobby Jones the supreme defensive forward for the Philadelphia Seventy-Sixers is a fine example of someone who through efficient running usually catches and blocks the player he is after.

If at the end of your practice you feel you need additional work on your running you can practice, as the Seventy-Sixers do, an exercise called "Seventeens." After practice and prior to the post-practice warm-down the players run the width of the court seventeen times. If you are concerned about your endurance intensity check it following this exercise using the aforementioned endurance guideline.

A Journey to the Canadian Arctic
Iqaluit, Nunavut (Canadian Arctic 63.4 5 N, 68.31 W)

<u>Friday, August 31, 2001</u>

We set our feet onto the Arctic on Tuesday, August 28, 2001. The mayor of Iqaluit met us at the airport and escorted us to our new residence. The mayor is also a Real Estate/Rental Agent in town. Our home is very nice for Arctic standards. It is a fairly new, triplex, owned by the Anglican Church, located in the center of town, with a wonderful view of Frobisher Bay. It has three bedrooms and a bathroom upstairs, large kitchen/dining and living spaces downstairs, with another bathroom and plenty of closet space. The apartment is unfurnished except for some kitchen items that were left by a previous tenant. With the help of our neighbor, an Anglican Captain in training and his wife, we were able to borrow some items to make the living space quite comfortable. I was also able to create some furniture items from "stuff" that was left by the previous tenant. It is amazing what one can do with cardboard boxes and linens. Fortunately we brought blow-up beds, sleeping bags and sheets. We are sleeping very well.

Our first full day was dedicated to getting our children, Zoé – Grade Six, and Parker – Kindergarten, into their respective schools. Both children have demonstrated outstanding courage and grace as we planned this journey and are bringing it to fruition. Zoé bravely entered her new school, the Aqsarniit (Northern Lights) Middle School, and has already made several new friends. Some of her new friends are Inuit girls who live in our neighborhood. Sadly many of their home situations are less than ideal. Even though our home is quite lovely, it is surrounded by small, government owned, pre-fabricated homes. As we proceed on our journey I am sure we will come closer to, and understand better, the biographies of those who live near and around us. The glory of Zoé's friendships is that so far any difference does not seem to matter. We can all learn a great deal from the wonder and innocence of our youth. She and her friends are bused to school at 8:05, bused home for lunch at 11:30, return after lunch at 12:30, and are dismissed at 3:30. It has been fun having her home each day for lunch.

Parker started Kindergarten on Thursday at the Nakasuk School. Our home actually overlooks his school. The school is a large, white, alien structure that looks as though it simply landed from some "other" place in the center of town. His eyes have been as large as polar bear eyes as he experiences his new life world. For example, yesterday I discovered the skin and partial carcass of a caribou across the street from our home. At first I did not know if it was a dog, a seal, or what. Someone had obviously harvested the caribou and dumped the remains on the street. We notified our neighbors from the church and our other neighbor in the tri-plex, the priest, a fifty-plus year old Inuit, now has the skin stretched under the building. To me the dumping of the skin was an early and clear reminder of the struggles between the traditional and the modern that exist amongst the Inuit. Inuit elders, like our neighbor, would have never thought of discarding the skin. The skin is simply too valuable for comfort, clothing and shelter. Modern Inuit on the other hand, bombarded by images of Nike and Calvin Klein, might not see the value in preserving the skin. Parker was quite captivated by the whole experience.

One additional household item that was lent to us was a small, color television and VCR. Being in the Arctic it only works if attached to the satellite-cable system. We hooked-up yesterday and it is amazing to receive 50-60 channels from Southern Canada and the United States. There can be no doubt that this square box adds significantly to

the confusion that swirls in the spirits of the Inuit. While one end of
their spirit is firmly rooted in the traditional the other is caught-up in a
whirlwind of images screaming of "American" materialism.

Why are we here? I have asked myself this question many times.
Why have we made this radical change? (Radical – from the Latin
radix, to get to the root of).

We came to the arctic to better understand ourselves, our world,
and for me, to try to get to the root of the phenomenons we call games
and sport. For as long as I can remember I have been involved with
games, sport, and dance. In addition to an active life and career in
each, I have also written widely about this journey, most recently in the
manuscript, *Running With Zoé: Conversations on the Meaning of Play,
Games, and Sport.*

Simply stated, I am here because I have a deep desire to try to get
to the root of our fascination (obsession) with games and sport. My
goal is to journey back in order that we may move forward. In other
words, I am going to attempt to better know and understand the roots
of traditional games to try to gain some insights into our fixation with
modern sport.

We also came to the Arctic so that our family can better understand
the world and our place in it. Joe Robinson in the *The Utne Reader*
(one of our favorites) talks about these personal journeys.

He says,

> *From our brains to our big toes, natural selection designed
> us to move, discover and seek out nourishment for both the
> body and our insatiably curious spirit. Real travelers today
> are in pursuit of the original sources, in this case, places that
> haven't been sanitized, ordered and commodified by modern
> civilization. As we get nearer to these sources we uncover
> deeper rhythms, which anchor us to something more than the
> next home entertainment purchase. Graham Greene called
> this a hankering for "a stage further back," a "nostalgia for
> something lost." He hit on the heart of the matter, because
> the drive to live an authentic life is one of the strongest of our*

> *psychological needs. Denial or distortion of authenticity causes neurosis. When we're authentic, we're in sync with the world around us. This sense of harmony opens us to the realm of the sacred, where the discordant, the dissonant, the incomplete, the disparate, the conflicted come together in resolution. It's the goal of all of the world's major religions under a variety of names: oneness, Nirvana, peace. And it's what every pilgrim, every personal explorer, seeks (Robinson, p. 64-69).*

Monday, September 3, 2001

'Tis early on Labor Day. Canada also celebrates this holiday. The town of Iqaluit is quiet as many folks have this day off from work and school. I will begin by sharing the events of the past few days.

Friday was without a doubt our official christening here in Iqaluit. In the evening we attended a workshop on traditional Inuit throat singing, held in conjunction with the Cultural Arts Programs for the Arctic Winter Games. Three Inuit elders from Nunavik (Northern Quebec) are teaching the weeklong workshop. Their names are Mary, Nellie, and Alacie. One goal of Elizabeth's journey to the north was to study throat singing. She was delighted that we could participate in the workshop as one could not ask for a more authentic classroom. In addition to our family of four, there were six or seven others in attendance, most young Inuit women, grade eight through ten. The young women were actually quite good at throat singing. They are very interested in this traditional form of song, and practice with each other regularly.

There was not much of an introduction to the class. None of the three teachers spoke English and only one of the participants/students spoke fluent Inuktitut. The elders began by motioning for one of us to stand-up one at a time, face them directly, hold their hands and arms, look deeply into their eyes, and imitate their sounds. There was no need for words. This class was about learning through imitation (play). The sounds the elders made came from deep within their throats; they hardly moved their mouths whatsoever. The most basic sound was "ohp-muh," repeated at a steady pace. The pupil started and then the elder entered on the opposite sound. For example while I was singing, "ohp," she was singing "muh." As you progressed the elder began to move her shoulders up and down and sway her torso side to side. The movements coincided with the sounds and song. One could not help but become one with the motion. If you could keep your senses and keep this going it was actually wonderfully hypnotic. One at a time an elder would simply stand up, motion for one of us to participate and off we went. When I say "off," I mean this not only literally but also spiritually. What was also interesting was that there was little communication between the elders. Much like players on a team, they were "in-touch" with each other on some "other" level and did not need words to coordinate their performance. This same deep intuition was also evident during their individual instruction. Elizabeth for example, who has a beautiful singing voice, was a very serious and passionate student. At one point in her lesson, Mary told Elizabeth (translated by one of the young Inuit women) to close her eyes, relax, and imagine the sound moving in her throat. Mary had a profound and faithful understanding of imagery and its relationship to learning. The elder's personal insights into teaching and learning were extraordinary.

During the session I asked Chevonne, a young Inuit woman who spoke Inuktitut and was one of the participants, to ask the elders about the meanings of their song. They explained and she translated that primarily women in pairs or threes do throat singing, often when the men were away hunting. Many of the sounds imitate animal sounds such as the gull and the goose. In addition to entertainment the singing can be a game, a polite competition where two women sing facing one another and the first to lose their concentration or laugh must sit down. Another woman then stands up and challenges the winner. This singing game can go on for long periods of time. It creates wholesome entertainment that helps to pass the time during the long winter months. It also helps to keep one warm as you move and breathe with one another. The elders emphasized in their explanation that the game between the girls and women was only for fun, no "one-up-person-ship." What was absolutely beautiful about this first night was watching the young Inuit women learn from their elders. The lessons affirmed for me the importance of "episodic learning." The elders, using touch, sound, and sight created a learning environment that was extremely meaningful. They were teaching on a very sophisticated level. Little did the elders know that the most cutting-edge scientists researching learning and memory have validated their pedagogy. Modern science tells us that because memory is a biologic process (excretion of biochemicals in the brain create the synaptic nerve connections that facilitate memory), the memories that are the most memorable are those that result from the profound events of our lives when the biochemical excretion in our brain is most extreme. Why then do so many in education discount participatory learning in favor of static, non-episodic, rote learning? I offer that no written test could assess the learning and understanding that took place when these young women stood face to face with an elder, looked into their eyes, held their hands and arms, and imitated their sounds and movement. It was a beautiful event.

Following our first class on throat singing we walked down the hill from Inuksuk High School to the Anglican Church Fellowship Hall. On this night there was a feast and dance for the community. Before we walked into the rear door we could smell the aroma of raw meat. Elizabeth commented that it reminded her of the meat lockers she visited during her youth in South Dakota. On entering our focus went immediately to a large blue tarp spread out on the floor that was covered with raw caribou (tuktu, "took-too"), seal (natsig, "nat-sirk"), and arctic char (iqalug, "e-kalug"). Piles of meat and innards were placed on large squares of cardboard that covered the tarp like pieces to a puzzle. Walking through the maze were two women cutting the meat into smaller pieces with their ulu knives (a half-moon shaped knife with a wooden or antler handle). Parker again had polar bear eyes as he witnessed this traditional Inuit pot luck supper. We had already had our supper so we passed on sharing in the feast. I am sure that as our journey proceeds we will take part in such festivals. Of the hundred or so in attendance we were four of only seven qallunaat (Inuktitut term for people who are non Inuit - anyone who comes to the North from the South). The Inuit made us feel perfectly welcome. We remained after supper and took in the games, music and dance.

The dance that followed the supper was a wonderful introduction to dance in the Arctic for Elizabeth and me. Both of us have an interest in the traditional drum dancing and social dances of the Inuit. Accompanying the dance was a four-piece band that played a form of Irish folk music. The dancing was a blend of Irish jig and step dancing. History tells us that these forms of music and dance were introduced to the Arctic by early (1600-1900) European whalers, explorers, and fur traders. During the dance there were also organized games for young and old alike. One dance/game required the dancers to quickly congregate into groups each time the music stopped. A member of the band would call out the number of people per group. Any person without a group had to sit down. It was an exciting game and it certainly helped to create community and friendship amongst all of the participants. In only three short days we had already been introduced to and practiced, two wonderful Inuit games, and dance.

On Sunday we went to the Anglican Church service and the fellowship that followed. The Anglican Church is a significant part of the Iqaluit community. Most Inuit have, over time, converted to Christianity. The church building is a dome-shaped, igloo structure in the center of town. The inside is quite appealing with large wooden beams that are directed skyward. The union of the beams forms the frame for a large skylight at the peak of the building. The altar of the church is draped with scenes of traditional Inuit life, surrounded by communion rails made from qamutiks ("kha-mo-teek," a wooden sled pulled by dog teams or snow machines). On Sunday there are three services, one in English and two in Inuktitut. While in church I experienced a certain level of discomfort when I thought of the church organized, government sponsored residential schools that attempted to squeeze out of Inuit youth, as if they were sponges, any remembrance of their traditions. I am however, able to set these personal feelings aside and participate as best as I can in the moment.

For our family, attending church is not something we do on a regular basis.

One after all, does not need to attend church regularly to have faith. Our family for example, chooses to express our faith in many ways: from our song and dance performance, both liturgical and in concert, to our teaching and scholarly work, to our fellowship with family and friends, to our respect for and preservation of our planet, to our respect for powers not in our control, to the respect and honor we have for those who have come before, to our journey to the Canadian Arctic. Richard Dawkins describes our faith as Religious non-believers.

The apartment we rent in Iqaluit is owned by the Anglican Church and we are grateful to have a centrally located, warm, and comfortable living space. One reason we went to church was for the fellowship and to say thank you to the members of the church who arranged for us to rent the apartment at a reduced rate ($2000.00 vs. $2700.00 Canadian Funds).

During the fellowship that followed the service I met some very interesting people from the North. One in particular was a qallunaat high school teacher named Dick. Dick and his wife have been in the North nearly thirty years. He and I began talking about television and the impact "the box" has had on the North. He said that television started in the 1970's with video taped replays of "Hockey Night in Canada" and "Dallas" that were flown or shipped in. Later satellite technology enabled live transmission of the CBC (Canadian Broadcasting Corporation). Today cable access provides 35-60 channels while home satellite dishes allow for 200 channels. He went on to say that prior to television there was no overwhelming sense amongst the less fortunate Inuit that they were indeed less fortunate. Without any comparisons they seemed content with their lifestyles. With television, he said, came all of the materialism of the South, i.e., fancy automobiles, showy clothing, extravagant houses, etc. Almost overnight some Inuit began to express feelings of low self esteem and self- worth. With a flip of a switch their spirits were altered forever.

Dick said that with television also came the introduction of hockey. He said that at the same time the Inuit sense of self-worth was being diminished so too was their sense of fair play. Young Inuit began to imitate the aggression exhibited on television from "Hockey Night in Canada." He said the change in local sport was sudden and profound. Throughout Iqaluit youth sport teachers and coaches noticed more physical contact, aggression, and less sportsmanship. While Dick was sharing his personal insights about sport I was immediately reminded of my supper last spring at Harvard with the Premiere of Nunavut, Paul Okalik. Premiere Okalik was in Cambridge, Massachusetts giving a speech on Nunavut. During the supper that followed at the Harvard Faculty Club, the conversation turned to sport and Premiere

Okalik talked unreservedly about his participation in hockey and the enjoyment he gets from a "good, hard" hit.

After church on Sunday we decided to venture down the Road To Nowhere. Yes, there is actually a road that leads out of town that is named the Road To Nowhere. We were told that as you proceed down the road you can go on either side, walk through the soft tundra and pick crow and blue berries. Crowberries, a favorite of the Inuit, are black and plump. Their many seeds give them a rather gritty taste. The blueberries, on the other hand, are slightly larger than the crowberries, but much sweeter in taste. We did not have to walk far before we came to a place with many berry plants. The tundra was quite interesting. It is soft in many places and up close reveals many varieties of plant life. Both the crow and blue berries grow close to the ground. The harvesting takes time as the berries are small and require fine motor skills to pick. After about two hours we had three to four cups of berries. Parker and Zoé especially enjoyed picking the berries; they were reminded of summer when we pick wild raspberries and thimbleberries at our cottage on Bois Blanc Island in Lake Huron in Michigan. There is something very authentic about eating a fresh berry pie or having fresh berries on pancakes when you know that you have gathered the fruit from the land. Parker actually had a difficult time sharing his stash as each berry was very special to him. While I was picking I was re-living the world of gatherers from throughout history. I imagined women with children on their backs and other children nearby spending long hours on the tundra in search of food to nurture their families and communities - how vitally important their efforts were to the survival of the family and community. Without their efforts we would never have survived as a species, since hunting, the men's arena of food support, was always a game of chance.

Inuit children grow up with a strong sense of belonging. This sense came from tightly woven bonds with family, friends, and the world around them. The bonds were made easily because of their frequent connections through play. Play for Inuit was how they learned about themselves and their world. It was fundamental to their learning of language, their relationship to others, their relationship to the environment (survival), and their relationship to a "higher" power. Sadly, the Christian Church did everything in their power to squeeze out of them any sense of belonging and, Get Rid Of It All.

One very positive outcome from our journey to the Arctic has been the self- directed play of our children. Because we were limited in the amount of "stuff" we could bring, Zoé and Parker have created and made all sorts of things. Most of their creations have a genuine nearness to the life-world they are living in. They have written and illustrated stories, carved soap, beaded, baked bannock, and sewn sealskins. Most of their play was voluntary and self-directed. Elizabeth and I simply provided the various materials and they did the rest. Their actions affirm the importance of play for young children. If given the opportunity, children will create things that satisfy their need for interaction, communication, knowing, and understanding. Moreover, their creations have real meaning to their present "state" of being. I have noticed this same self-directed play from the Inuit children near our home. Despite the cold they are often out of doors, making snow angels, building snow houses, hitting snowballs, ice climbing, and snow sliding.One of Parker's creations is a story entitled, <u>The Whale Watching Family</u>. I am going to include the text of his story so that you can share in his playful pleasures.

The Whale Watching Family

By: Parker Kilbourne (Six years old)
"We are going off to our summer camp. How fun!
We are going away from our beach to our whale watching camp.
We are out on the sea whale watching.
This is our igloo camp in the winter.
We are going on a sled ride pulled by our dog.
We just got back from our ride. The End."

One of Many Awakenings

In Harold Cardinal's influential best selling book, <u>The Unjust</u> <u>Society</u> he talks about people like Elizabeth and myself and our interest in First Nation's people:

> *It is time for concerned whites to reassess their involvement in a deep and honest manner so that their interest may become more meaningful to the native people. The hard truth remains that the responsibility for the revitalization of the Indian society falls upon the shoulders of the Indian people and no one else (Cardinal, p. 78).*

Harold Cardinal's observations have really made me think about our involvement with the Inuit in the Arctic. Cardinal suggests that our energies should be directed towards the enlightenment of ourselves and other non-native:

> *There exists a great need for knowledge in the white society about Indians and similarly a need in the Indian communities for more information about white society. Indian leaders stand ready to outline to whites the difficulties they see facing their people and to explain their own solutions. Interested whites can get this sort of information and pass it on to their own communities. As interest and understanding grow, as Indian-educated non-Indians educate their own people, more intelligent assessments can be made, more intelligent help*

> *offered. The kind of help and information Indians encountering white society need will then be more readily available. A basis for mutual understanding can develop (Cardinal, p. 80).*

Harold Cardinal provided me with a much needed rousing and re-evaluation of our time in Iqaluit. I think what he suggests may be our most important assignment. We must learn as much as we can about the life-world of the Inuit so that we can pass this information on to our own communities. As I said earlier, the most important component of the sharing is that we have first hand experiences. Hopefully our added knowledge and experiences will provide the groundwork for greater understanding. Towards that end I think our journey so far has been successful. We have spent many hours reading the literature of and living with the people of the North. We are truly researching the "lived experience." Every member of our family has learned more than my words can ever hope to express.

Monday Morning, September 10, 2001

Today is quite overcast, rainy and cold. In the distance one can see the beginnings of a blanket of snow. It will not be long before the blanket weaves its way to Iqaluit.

Each night when I go to bed my mind is flooded with memories and thoughts about the day. This journey is truly amazing. I am so fortunate to have a sabbatical where I can focus my energies on studying and researching lived experience. What has been a special bonus is that we are able to do this as a family, a family sabbatical. Both Elizabeth and I get great joy from witnessing our children share this journey. Zoé for example, is working diligently on a science project about climate change and the impact it is having on the Arctic. Through her I have learned about the impact our (United States of America) pollution is having on the polar bears of the Arctic. Her younger brother Parker (his new nickname is mosquito because he is constantly buzzing around his sister) is collecting rocks to build Inuksuks. Inuksuks are markers built from large stones that were/are used to designate locations and direct energies, both human and animal (caribou). One may think of them as almost an arctic lighthouse.

Saturday morning we received our first Foodmail order. Foodmail is a program where you can order groceries from Montreal or Ottawa and they are shipped via airfreight to the Arctic. If the items are what they call, "good food," i.e., fruits, vegetables, dairy, meat, etc., the Canadian Government helps to subsidize the freight. The participating store's advertising flyers arrive on Friday. The orders must then be faxed by Monday, paid for with a credit card for arrival the following Saturday. On Saturday Parker and I walked to the airport, picked-up our four boxes and hired a cab for the ride home. It was so exciting to unpack the boxes and have kiwi, oranges, apples, broccoli, a whole chicken, and cheese. Wow!

Between Foodmail and the Sealift (pre-purchased food and staples that are shipped in cargo containers), folks in the Arctic somehow manage the high cost of living. As is usually the case, those that "have" (credit cards, available money to prepay for the Sealift) benefit most. Those that "don't have" must pay.

Nine Eleven – Too Far Away

September 13, 2001

Today the hills surrounding Iqaluit are glistening with a wash of sunshine. We like many, have put on hold some of the proceedings of our lives because of the tragic events in the United States. It may be several days before we emerge from this dark cloud of humanity and return to our task here in the Arctic. We will, however, emerge with an even stronger commitment to try to make sense of, and understand, our diverse world. This after all, is the reason we are in the Arctic.

The terrorist attacks of September 11th in United States have been very difficult to explain to Zoé and Parker. Zoé has listened to and watched the horror of the tragedy unfold, asked many relevant questions, and is writing her thoughts in her journal. Tuesday she had a very moving moment in school after learning of the events. When she returned from lunch her teacher shared the catastrophe of the terrorist attack in America with her class. She then asked Zoé, the only American in her school, if she had anything she wanted to say. Zoé said, "It is very hard," and began to cry. Her tears provided a much-needed lesson in the "commonness" that unites all of us. Her sorrow pulled both qallunaat and Inuit together. That night she wrote the following in her journal.

> *Basically I am scared and very nervous. I wish I had my dog and I am just praying that everything will be all right. Well, leaving now sad and scared. I hope for Peace, Peace, Peace, Peace and just Peace and Love.*

It has been interesting to be in another country, so far from home, and away from family and friends, during this tragedy. First and foremost, family and friends provide comfort in times of great disaster. In addition, there is a common bond one has with others when you are in your home country. Here, we are basically alone when it comes to family, friends and fellow Americans. I think we may be the only Americans in Iqaluit, or so it seems.In Iqaluit, life seems to move forward without much discussion of the events in the United States. I went to the local store, post office and bank yesterday and did not overhear one person talking about the attack on America.

As I think about the events in America I am filled with many questions. Besides my heartfelt sadness and grief for the loss of so many innocent lives, I find myself asking over and over again, why? What has America done, or for that matter not done, to generate this much hate for our citizens? And, will the extreme retaliation proposed by our Government leaders bring any meaningful and lasting resolution? I will not go any further with this at the moment. I do however want to share a few questions I have about the role of games and sport in all of this. One may ask, "Why Games and Sport?"

Yesterday I listened to an interview with the highly respected and informed sport journalist, Frank Deford. Mr. Deford is a Senior Writer for *Sports Illustrated* and a regular contributor to *National Public Radio*. He was asked about the postponement of professional sporting events because of the events in New York City, Washington D.C. and Pennsylvania. He began his answer with a brief discussion about similar postponements at the beginning of World War II, and after the assassinations of President Kennedy and Martin Luther King Jr. He compared this current tragedy to those events and said that America needs to return to some sense of normalcy. He went on to say that sport provides that normalcy. I have tremendous respect for Mr. Deford, but must respectively disagree. To me, professional sport today is anything but "normal."

Professional sport at the beginning of WWII (1941) and in the 1960s is very different from sport of today. During the 1940s, 1950s, 1960s, and even into the 1970s, sport was not the huge business (commodity) it is today. During those years it was still possible for an average American, individual or family, to attend a live sporting event. Players were not making two-hundred to seven-hundred times the salaries of entry-level schoolteachers or firefighters. Sport still had a genuine nearness to our citizenry. In addition, sport was not the hypnotic spectacle it has become. Simply stated, televised sport and the money it provided had not yet arrived.

I think that during this time of catastrophe and heartbreak, America needs to turn-off and turn away from the lavish spectacles of professional sport. We need to spend meaningful time helping our families and friends deal with, understand, and learn from the events of this week. We need normalcy on the human level, not the spectacle that sport has become. Human normalcy cannot happen if sixty million spectators (a spectator is someone who watches a lavish pubic show) are glued to their television sets watching the National Football League.

The spectacle of modern games and sport has moved us far away from the reality of our world. I include under this umbrella the new, made for television programs such as "Survivor" and "The Mole." We have become so preoccupied, almost obsessed with game and sport spectacles, that we have lost sight of the world around us. Did this collective disconnection have anything to do with the attacks on the people of New York City and Washington D.C? I believe that on some level it did.

According to the ongoing investigation the perpetrators of these horrific attacks were trained as pilots in our flight training schools, lived in our neighborhoods, and shopped in our grocery stores. To think that nobody took the time and effort to discover on a familiar (family) level just who these folks were and what they might be up to. Were we simply too preoccupied with our lavish public shows, i.e., modern day bread & circus (Rome)? Keep people fed and entertained and they will not pay attention.

One early lesson that I am discovering about traditional games versus modern games is that America's present obsession with lavish spectacles simply did not exist for the Inuit. Games for the Inuit were far more human in nature and were intimately linked to the well being of their families and communities. Everyone, including elders, men, women, and children had a role. The survival of each depended upon honest and sincere communication, cooperation and shared reciprocity. In other words, these notions of humanness were far more significant than being entertained by lavish public displays.

These past few days, needing a break from the satellite television coverage of the tragic events in the United States, I have been watching the informative and authentic series of films entitled, *Netsilik Eskimos: The People of the Seal.* Hugh Brody (2000) says, "The Netsilit films are arguably the most complete documentary of hunter-gatherer life ever made, and they provide a unique window onto the material life, economic activities, and human qualities of the Inuit (Brody, p. 302)."

What is plainly obvious from these films are the human qualities of early Inuit. Could we have avoided this week's senseless tragedy in America had we been more "in- touch" with one another? Were we simply, "Too Far Away?" *(Chapter V)*. Again, I have so many questions.

As I proceed to search for the deeper meanings of games in the Arctic I will elaborate extensively on the communication, cooperation and shared reciprocity of the Inuit. My current reflections are merely an introduction based upon the events that unfolded in the United States this past Tuesday.

On a happier note, today is Parker's birthday. He is now six years old. He has let both Elizabeth and I know that he wants a Skidoo (snow machine) for his birthday. This past year he saved all of his gift money and used it as partial payment for a small boat and motor for our summer home on Bois Blanc Island, Michigan. Having achieved this goal he now has his mind set on a snow machine. This morning he woke up with a small fever and cough so he did not attend school. We think the changes in his life world, i.e., kindergarten, growth spurt, and a new home and community may have taxed his well being. Tonight we will celebrate with our first cake in the Arctic, chocolate of course. We will try to make six candles so that there will be fire and a wish accompanying his birthday celebration.

Friday, September 14, 2001

Today is another beautiful sunny day in Iqaluit. As the sunshine washes over Iqaluit a blanket of snow slowly weaves its way down the nearby hills. The chill in the air is more obvious each day.

The tragedy in America pulls ever so powerfully on our spirits. Today in Iqaluit there will be an outside prayer vigil at noon at the Anglican Church. We will join the many citizens of the world and remember those that have died. We will also offer our prayers for healing and for a more humane future.

At this time I find it very difficult to concentrate on our journey to the Arctic. I am filled with so many emotions and thoughts. Again, why are we here? I think the tragic events in America somehow have a connection to our move to the north.

We moved here because we were looking for greater authenticity in our lives. For me, I am searching for meaningful authenticity in modern games and sport, a mirror of American life. Thinking about sport (Sport Philosophy) after all, is my primary field of inquiry.

Some of the worries I have about modern sport are that it seems more and more, out of control and completely, removed from reality. How can we justify paying one athlete an amount equal to the salaries of 700 firefighters? Who are the real heroes? Who are more important: the legions of millionaire athletes who bombard our airways with lavish displays of sport excellence, or everyday folks who teach our children, fight our fires, help our sick, and protect our environment?

One troubling aspect of modern sport and all of its trappings, from advertising to open displays of violence, is what it is doing to our children. The, "win-at-all-cost" and "king-of-the-hill" mentalities so prevalent in modern sport, are teaching our children that winning, no matter the human cost, is all that matters. Nowhere is this attitude more evident than with the epidemic of doping and substance abuse that surrounds all of sport. Some of my college students, when asked about the use of drugs to enhance athletic performance, see no problems whatsoever. They sometimes refer to celebrated professional athletes who have enhanced their performance with such drugs, as their role models. Modern sport has created an artificial bubble that has engulfed far too many Americans. We have become hypnotized into thinking that we all need to be associated on some level. We buy the hats, shoes, and jerseys. We spend hours in front of our televisions, completely removed from the world around us, fixated on events that have very little to do with our everyday survival. We look up to professional athletes as if they somehow are more enlightened and know more than any of us. Once, while lobbying for education programs for professional athletes, I had a National Basketball Association coach say to me, "Do you really think that they (the athletes) will listen? In their minds they are far smarter than you because even though you have many years of college and experience, they make more money." The bubble is huge and far too many Americans have been sucked in.

Monday September 17, 2001

This morning we awoke to an Iqaluit that we have not seen before. The bay was sheltered with a thick fog. One could hardly see the shoreline. As I made my way through town doing errands, an icy mist washed over my face.

We are still ill at ease from the events in America. We are like four arctic ravens searching for wind. Our wind will return, just when, we cannot predict.

Elizabeth and I both have discomfort over the tornado of anger and rage that seems to be sweeping across America. I hope and pray that we (Americans) do not become "them." Inuit elders talk often about this. One such story is when an Inuk named Paulusi was caught throwing live dogs into a fire. Shortly after, Paulusi was severely injured by fire. On Friday we attended an outdoor service at the Anglican Church to honor those who have been killed and to send our prayers to their families and loved ones. It was incredibly healing to be in the presence of both Inuit and qallunaat. The service was in both Inuktitut and English. Together we sang and prayed. "Amazing Grace" sung simultaneously in Inuktitut and English was breathtaking. What was so magnificent about the service was that the duality allowed each person to find his or her native path to compassion and understanding. The success was an affirmation that meaningful bridges can be built between disparate folks. It also confirmed that at our core humans are caring and compassionate beings.

When we arrived home Parker shared the artwork that he had done that morning in kindergarten. His class was working on the alphabet letter "A." His teacher asked each student to draw pictures of things that start with "A." Parker's "A" pictures included an injured person in an <u>A</u>mbulance with an <u>A</u>ngel overhead. Children do listen, children do see, and children do have profound understanding. Saturday morning we worked together with 150-200 folks from Iqaluit to help clean up the bay. The amount of litter that was gathered was astonishing. What was even more amazing was just what the litter consisted of. Everything from the fresh innards, legs and hooves of caribou, the collar and skeleton of a dog, rotting seals, soiled diapers, glass, tires, wood of all sizes and shapes, large cans, hundreds of plastic bottles and pop cans - it was another one of those Polar Bear eye moments.

Following our clean-up efforts on the bay we proceeded to the local curling rink for the Iqaluit Recreation Department sign-ups for fall activities. The sign-ups were an enormous event. There were literally hundreds of folks lined-up at tables signing up themselves and their children up for everything from soccer to Greenhouse Club.

Sunday, September 23, 2001

The snow has arrived. Today we awoke to a cascade of snow flurries. While it is snowing in Iqaluit, friends remind me that it is 25 degrees Celsius at home. As I wrote today's date I was reminded that today is the birthday of my late sister Janett. A drunk driver tragically killed Janett eighteen years ago. The accident happened on July 4th, 1983, three weeks after the parade that celebrated the Basketball Championship of the 1983 Philadelphia Seventy-Sixers. One moment I was at the "summit" of bliss, the next I was near the "base" of sorrow.

During my previous entry I introduced the relationship of traditional Inuit to their life world on the land. One important aspect of this relationship was their connection to the animals they hunted. Inuit feel that they can communicate with every living animal. They speak the same language and thus were able to live as equal partners in the same world. George Kuptana says, "In the beginning animals did communicate with people. It was told that in the beginning of first man, every living creature spoke, including humans, caribou, lemmings, mosquitoes (Pelly, 2001, p. 33)."

In addition to their communicative capabilities, Inuit can also transform themselves into other living animals. Depending upon the circumstances, Inuit could become other animals while at the same time animals could transform themselves into human forms. This was shared reciprocity at the deepest level. These transformative and communicative capabilities were at the heart of the reverence Inuit had for animals and the environment. Any harm to others would actually harm themselves.

What can we learn from the Inuit's ancient traditions of communication and transformation? Might it be beneficial for us at certain times to be like traditional Inuit where, depending upon the circumstances, we actually "walk in the shoes" of another, whether that be another human or another animal. Could this transformation bring *real* meaning to our understanding of our diverse world?

Since my major field of inquiry is games and sport, I often think of transformation and professional sport. Professional sport as I said earlier, seems too far away to facilitate any *real* nearness. There is not much likelihood of sincere transformation. How can we relate to an athlete, of which there are hundreds, who earn such astronomical amounts of money? In my work in professional basketball I have often been in the company of these multimillionaires. I always have many questions. The one question that I always ask is, "What have we done to create this great distance?"

Only last week the New York Mets baseball team donated their paychecks from one game to the victims of the tragedy in New York. The amount donated was reported to be $500,000. If you multiply this amount by the 162 game-season, you get a total of $81,000,000 (eighty-one million dollars). That amount equals the approximate salaries of 1700 firefighters or teachers. As a teacher/professor myself, how can I relate, yet alone hope to transform?

The aforementioned distance simply did not exist with the Inuit. A nearness to others and their world, so important to their survival, was the nucleus of their life. This equity is best demonstrated in the scheme they designed to distribute the meat and oil from a successful hunt. The meat and oil would be divided into equal amounts and then each pile was placed in the shape of a large circle. With a designated hunter's back turned to the piles, he would blindly distribute each pile of food. In this way he assured that the distribution was fair and equitable (See Appendix).

And then, there is the respect the Inuit have for their environment. For example, the Inuit always pour a small amount of fresh water into the mouth of a dead seal. They feel that seals are always searching for fresh water and by sharing a small amount with the dead seal they can help them complete their journey. This act of reverence helped insure a plentiful supply of seals, thus helping to preserve the survival of their families and communities. How often do we take the time to think about how and from where our food comes from, and moreover like the seals, where it might want to go? I always ask my college students to think about this at Thanksgiving. I say, "I want you to think about how the turkey you will eat on Thanksgiving came into the world. Think about the person who fed it good food and water. Think about the person who harvested it and prepared it for cooking. Think about the person who transported the turkey to market. Think about the person who then sold it. Think about the person who dressed it and prepared it for eating. And then, think about the amount of time it takes you to gobble it down. Where is the moment when you pay your respect to not only the turkey, but to the many folks who helped to facilitate your existence? Where is the moment of transformation when you, like the Inuit, become *One* with the animal?" Being *One* with anything may sound silly to some. If we were truly *One* with others, might we have averted the recent misfortune in America?

Yesterday we went on a long refreshing walk to Iqaluit's cemetery and then onto the Rotary Club carnival at the curling rink. All three, the walk, the cemetery, and the carnival were nourishing.

The cemetery overlooks a beautiful stretch of the bay. It is surrounded on one side by a large rocky hill. The simple graves were mounds of dirt, some surrounded by rocks or small fences, all with a simple wooden cross at the head. Most of the crosses had the names and ages of the deceased. Many graves had dried flowers and small offerings. As you walked towards the older section of the cemetery the crosses became more weathered and broken. I could not help but think of the many lives of the people who had been buried here. I also thought about the reverence of their final resting place, people of the land and sea, so near once again.

From the cemetery we walked along the bay towards the curling rink. The Iqaluit Rotary Club was holding their annual carnival to raise money for the community. The event was a huge success. There were many people enjoying the games and festivities, both qallunaat and Inuit. The games were simple carnival games, ball toss, ring toss, etc. For one or more tickets (tickets were fifty cents each) you could test your skill at the various games. Prizes of small stuffed animals in three sizes were awarded on the basis of your success at each game. In addition to the games there was food; hot dogs, French fries, pop and candy. I particularly enjoyed the French fries. It has been along time since I had this American staple.

What was most affirming about the carnival and games was how popular it was for everybody. It provided a great atmosphere to get to know one another. At their core games are made of play, and one of the wonders of play is its ability to create bonds between other humans and their environment. What are the lessons from this event that we can apply to building more constructive bridges between the people of Iqaluit? One simple lesson is that games like these, games that are simple and affordable, need to take place more often.

Language & Transformation

September 24, 2001

I have been thinking a lot about the notion of transformation. What brought it back to my attention was Zoé's French class at the Aqsarniit Middle School.

Last week Zoé began studying French at school. She had her choice of French or Inuktitut. Her class meets two days per week, Monday and Wednesday. After her first lesson she came home for lunch, bounded in the door, and with a huge smile gleefully said, "Bonjour!" She was so excited. In only one day of lessons she was able to converse with Elizabeth who has studied some French. She had entered a new pathway of transformation. She told us that when she returns to Massachusetts she wants to continue studying French. If only these opportunities existed in our local public schools back home.

Language is a wonderful way for humans to transform themselves into the life worlds of others. Words, after all, create and describe our world. For the first time in her seven years of public education, Zoé has an opportunity to experience our world through the sounds, images and descriptions of a language other than English.

One responsibility I have as a college professor is to advise students in their course of study. A recurring dilemma for many of my students is the requirement that they successfully complete two years of a foreign language. Research in language acquisition clearly demonstrates that the most effective teaching and learning takes place when students are young, preferably before age eight. The pre-eight brain has far greater adaptability for language acquisition. Why then do we not dedicate the resources, both material and human, to teaching a second language when our children are ten or younger? It seems so simple. Zoé affirmed this when she said, "It just isn't fair. America needs to teach languages other than English when we are young." Bilingualism (transformation via language) is one more path to greater global understanding.

<u>September 25, 2001</u>

Today is another cold, overcast day in Iqaluit. The snow from the weekend has been melted by rain. The potholes in the streets are full of rainwater providing children with a maze for jumping and hopscotch. In the bay there sits another large ship filled with goods and materials for the long winter.

Darwin & Transformation

The Inuit's embodiment of transformation is a concept that may have significant meaning during this fragile time in our world. As I thought about transformation and the lessons one might learn from connecting with another, I was reminded of the valuable work of Charles Darwin. History and science demonstrate that Darwin's contributions to our understanding of the world are as important, if not more important, than the contributions of Galileo, Newton or Einstein.

> *There is grandeur in this view of life, with its several powers, having been originally breathed by the Creator into a few forms or into one; and that, whilst this planet has gone cycling on according to the fixed law of gravity, from so simple a beginning endless forms most beautiful and most wonderful have been, and are being evolved (Darwin, p. 490).*

The aforementioned statement is the last sentence in Charles Darwin's seminal work, <u>On The Origin of Species</u>. Little did he know that the theory of evolution he put forward in his "Tree of Life" design had been practiced by traditional Inuit for centuries. The Inuit's notion that we could transform ourselves into other living things, that somehow everything was connected, is precisely what Darwin said in his book. Modern DNA testing now confirms what Darwin theorized and what early Inuit knew, that every living thing, from the whales in the sea to the ravens overhead, are linked. We (humans) are united with other humans and every other living thing on this planet.

The recent horrific terrorist acts against innocent Americans were a clear and obvious declaration of the great dis-connection that exists between human beings. In other words, the healthy transformative connections that are necessary are simply not apparent. Somehow they have been made dormant. These disconnections create struggles: man versus the environment, hunger versus abundance, danger versus safety, poverty versus wealth, brown versus white, or Jesus versus Muhammad. The latter religion, is especially troubling. The attack on America demonstrated beyond belief, the power religion has in distancing one group of humans from another.

Inuit transformation, like Darwin's "Tree of Life," seems to make a great deal of sense. The idea of one Creator from so simple a beginning making all living things, each somehow connected to others, is truly most beautiful and wonderful. In these times of great distance it may be a notion we wish to transform to, or connect with.

The Transformation of Yankee Stadium

<u>September 26, 2001</u>

This past Sunday we spent the afternoon watching, "America's Prayer" from Yankee Stadium in New York City. The gathering was a multi-denominational prayer service for the missing, injured, and deceased in New York. At first I was skeptical about the service. As it proceeded I became a devoted admirer. The prayers, speeches, and music all served to unite the participants. The notion of a Large God, encompassing and connecting *All,* was the prevailing theme. It was Inuit transformation at its best. The location of the event, one of the most hallowed in all of sport, was the perfect venue for the service. The transformation of Yankee Stadium into a place of worship was a clear reminder of the deep connections that exist between religion, and games and sport.

For the Inuit there was no separation between games and religion. They were intimately linked.

Life for the Inuit was extremely hard. The world they inhabited was enormously unforgiving; the severe cold, sunless days, and harsh winds, a seemingly endless challenge. It was religion, their unified system of beliefs and practices relative to sacred things, that helped them make sense of these lifelong challenges. Religion provided answers to the unanswerable. Many of their questions focused on the availability of food sources.

Like most of the world's religions, the Inuit's system of beliefs and practices were unified around the following: 1.) Connection To Nature, 2.) Sacred Times, 3.) Sacred Places, 4.) Respect For Powers Not In Our Control, and 5.) Special People With Special Power.

Knowing & Understanding

September 28, 2001

Today the sun shines bright through a few scattered clouds. Yesterday we awoke to four inches of snow resting on the ground. The locals tell us that the snow, cold, and ice are here to stay. It is sobering to think that it will remain like this until late June. Elizabeth and I both felt a sense of release at seeing the snow covering the hills and ground. This after all, is the Arctic. Zoe and Parker thoroughly enjoy the snow around our home and on the nearby playground. Parker was early to school so he could help his school mates build a snow person.

Yesterday while listening to the local Inuktitut/English radio station, there was a warning of a Polar Bear in a neighborhood nearby. They said if you see the bear please call Wildlife Management and then do your best to scare it back onto the land. I looked at Elizabeth and said, "Great! I'll just go out and try to frighten the bear. Just how does one do that?"

Wednesday afternoon we hosted a small group of young Inuit women at our home. Elizabeth had agreed to help them with their throat singing performance. This coming Monday there is a throat singing competition at the Legislative Building, the "Ledge" as locals say, and these young high school women are participating. The afternoon workshop at our home proved to be very successful. Elizabeth provided a much-needed set of eyes and ears to assist the young women in polishing their performance skills. What was most interesting about their singing was how they worked with one another. At one difficult time one of the young women said to her partner, "I don't like you right now. You're usually not like this. You're usually much easier to work with." I overheard this exchange from the living room (they were practicing in the kitchen) and immediately noted the complete straight forwardness with which it was delivered. Honesty such as this is very common to Inuit.

Epistemology - The Study of the Nature of Knowing and Understanding:

How One Comes To Know and Understand

One of the reasons I have come to the Arctic is to investigate how the Inuit come to know and understand. In other words, who were the Inuit's teachers and how were they taught? Through my study of previous inquiries and pending interviews with Inuit, I hope to gain a greater understanding of these methods. I am interested in knowing and understanding as it relates to games.

Previous inquiries tell us that knowledge and understanding about games were organized bodies of wisdom that were passed on by fathers, mothers, close relatives or friends, and by the person's personal engagement with the land, sea, animals, songs, drumming and dance. Mark Nuttall (2000) explains in very plain language this process as it applied to hunting.

> *This knowledge (hunting) is not something which is simply acquired or accumulated out on the ice or at sea, or through the teachings of an experienced hunter. True, the novice hunter is instructed in basic hunting skills and the education of a hunter includes practical knowledge - instructions of where and how to hunt, how to handle boats, gear, rifles, and so on. The novice also learns precise rules for correct hunting and treatment of animals, and for sharing and dividing large marine or land animals. Hunting areas are essentially, "territories of knowledge," and in addition to good equipment and skill, knowledge about the movement, behavior and habits of animals is vital to their successful capture, as is the knowledge of good hunting places, and the names and stories associated with the landscape and the seascape. Becoming a hunter is more a result of situated learning, or learning in practice – hunters learn to identify with hunting territories of the locality, and to understand the movement and habits of seals and other animals, and the hunter's place in the wider social context (Nuttall, p. 42).*

The same situated learning techniques were used in games as well. Games were learned during small gatherings and ceremonies of clan members. The mode of transmission from adults to the young depended on the substance and purpose of the game. One's father, mother, brother, sister, or other family or community member, transmitted the games. The gatherings and ceremonies became the "territories of knowledge."

The more I read about the educational practices of the Inuit, the more I am reminded of John Dewey, the early twentieth century philosopher who was passionate about situated learning. Dewey called it "Instrumentalism or Experimentalism." I wonder if Dewey knew that the Inuit of the Arctic had been practicing this for centuries. I find it very interesting that both Charles Darwin and John Dewey were not alone in their knowing and understanding of evolution and education. In fact, they were both "Johnny Come Lately," when compared to the Inuit. Acknowledging the evolutionary and pedagogical wisdom of the Inuit is long overdue.

Modern education has not done a very good job of teaching the valuable lessons that can be learned from traditional people. Teachers expound and glorify the work of Charles Darwin, John Dewey and others while paying virtually no attention to the outstanding contributions of traditional folks like the Inuit. In my twenty-eight years of organized education, I leaned very little about the wisdom of traditional people. Maybe my teachers were ignorant or afraid of something? By honoring the ideas, phrases, and observations of someone unlike themselves, they would have to bare themselves and reveal a common-ness that connect us all. What is our fear of this common-ness? The irony in all of this is that at a very deep level, these connections are exactly what the Inuit, Charles Darwin, and John Dewey put forward.

I think the aforementioned fear can also be applied to modern games. Modern folks are afraid to think that just maybe modern games and sport are connected to the traditions of our past. They think of themselves and their games as civilized while portraying the practices of traditional people as somehow primitive and barbaric. I posit that there are far too many commonalities between modern games and traditional games to discount the connections. Like religion, the connections are deep and tightly woven through thousands of years of evolution. No amount of modern judgment will be able to unravel or tear these connections apart. Can we, by understanding these connections, gain greater understanding and appreciation for modern games? I think we can. That after all, is the reason we came to the Arctic.

September 30, 2001

It is Sunday morning and snowing once again. From our home I do not see any automobiles on the streets nearby. Yesterday they told us over the radio that we no longer needed to worry about the polar bear. They must have either scared it back on to the land or someone shot and killed it. If a polar bear is threatening your life you may shoot them in self-defense, otherwise you must obtain the proper permit to hunt a polar bear.

Before I return to writing about games, I want to mention another incident that demonstrated to me anyway, the distance that exists between qallunaat and Inuit in Iqaluit. Yesterday we took Parker to his gymnastics class at the Nakasuk School. Local instructors run a gymnastics program for children of various age groups on Saturday mornings. The classes are $25.00 (Canadian) for six to eight weeks of instruction. On the way to the school I noticed fifteen to twenty Inuit adults and children waiting in front of the John Howard Society building. The John Howard Society is similar to the Salvation Army. They provide food, clothing, and services for the disadvantaged. In our first month here I have never seen people lined-up near their building. In fact, we were told that the Fire Marshall had recently condemned the structure. I noted the gathering and we proceeded to the elementary school for Parker's class. Upon entering the gymnasium I immediately noticed that nearly all of the instructors and students were qallunaat. Was I surprised? Sadly, no. Elizabeth stayed at the class with Parker while Zoe and I went to the grocery store. On our way home, Zoé and I stopped and asked why people were waiting at the John Howard Society. We were told that they were waiting for someone to come, open the doors, and spread out the second-hand clothing. I am not sure if people had to purchase the clothing or if it was simply free. For me, the juxtaposition of the gymnastics class versus the folks at the John Howard Society was quite disturbing. Both groups of people were out-fitting their bodies, just in very different ways.

In the afternoon Zoé and I walked to her friend's house and then went on to the library. Zoé's friend, her single mom, and two siblings live in "White Row." White Row is a series of long white, tattered two story apartment buildings on the east side of Iqaluit. White Row is home to many in Iqaluit. Zoé's friend's mother works for the Department of Social Services and because of the housing shortage in Iqaluit, White Row was the only housing they could find. Their family is an amazing example of the braveness that exists in the Arctic. Their courageous spirits have taught us many lessons.

Now back to games. Yesterday, I had a revelation of sorts about games and sport. Thinking about religion, transformation, and situated learning, I came to the realization that modern games have powerful links to the pagan animism that guided us for most of our evolution. I use the word pagan with reservation because the word itself carries so much negative baggage. We have somehow become brain washed into thinking that pagan means, without religion. In fact, when you look up the word in the dictionary the first definition is, "heathen - a person who does not believe in an established religion." Were the beliefs of traditional Inuit not religious?

Modern games provide us with many meaningful connections to the "living thing" deep within all of us. Many refer to this as our inborn animism. Games bring us closer to nature, closer to one another, closer to the unimaginable, and closer to our collective will for continued existence. Lately, this animism has been particularly evident in the virtuosity of the great golfer Tiger Woods. Tiger, like great traditional

Inuit hunters, provides us with the hope that tomorrow will be a better day.

<u>October 2, 2001</u>

This morning I was greeted with seven messages on the Internet. As we continue our journey in the Arctic, hearing from family and friends provides great joy and comfort.

During the lunch hour yesterday we attended a Throat Singing Demonstration-Competition at the Legislative Building. Yesterday October 1st, was International Music Day. Folks throughout the world celebrated the wonder of music in all of its many forms. The wonderful transformative and healing characteristics of music provides great happiness to many. In these times of tremendous need, might we wish to play, or listen to our favorite music?

The "Ledge" is a modern building in the center of Iqaluit. The interior design is quite striking. The meeting hall is filled with traditional objects and art; a qamutik (sled), qulligs (oil lamps), carvings, and several beautiful woven tapestries. The chairs and gallery benches are covered with seal skins. Even the handles on the doors are traditional, having been made from walrus tusk and silver.

The Throat Singing event was truly "whole-some." The audience was both qallunaat and Inuit. As the event unfolded there was a feeling of genuine enthusiasm in the hall. After the introductions (Inuktitut and English), there was a demonstration of throat singing followed by the competition. The two young high school women whom Elizabeth had helped with their performance actually won First Prize. They were each awarded Arctic Winter Games sweatshirts. Elizabeth also performed and did very well. It was interesting to watch the reactions from the members of the audience as she sang with her partner. I think they were genuinely impressed.

One object that was centermost in the hall was the qullig. The qullig is a lamp carved from stone that holds oil to illuminate the dark and provides heat for warmth and cooking. They range in size from approximately eight to sixteen inches in length. Oil from seals, whales, walrus, polar bears, even caribou can be used in the qullig.

It was the women's responsibility to light and maintain the qullig. The oil and flame required faithful attention. Because the men were often on the land hunting, the survival of the family or clan depended on the women's devotion to the qullig. This is another example of the mutual reciprocity that existed between men and women. The notion of, "One-Up-MAN-ship," was not their way of thinking or doing. Carolyn Palliser in <u>Sinews of Survival</u> says,

> *To be an Inuk woman a couple of decades ago wasn't complicated, for gender roles were clearly defined and religiously followed to survive up North. You were a wife to your husband, a mother to your children, a housewife who cleans and cares for the animal skins and furs your husband brings back home from the hunt. You have dexterous skills which are essential for making clothes, for making transportation facilities and shelters, and you were trained at an early age (Issenman, p. 179).*

One can learn a great deal about human survival when one examines the harmonious relationships that existed between Inuit men and women. Theirs was an almost perfect union, defined and refined over hundreds of years. It allowed them to exist harmoniously in an incredibly unforgiving environment. Their mutual respect and understanding of one another provided the greatest opportunities for the survival of their children and themselves. In many parts of the world, including America, a revisiting of our understanding and practice of shared reciprocity is also long overdue.

Yesterday, Zoé got the "Okay" for her science project. She has decided to measure the particle air pollution in Iqaluit. One obvious environmental problem in Iqaluit is the disposal of garbage. For many years they have disposed of the garbage on the land or burned it in large fires. Because of the rocky ground and frost, landfill dumps are out of the question.

One of the major contributors to the garbage predicament in Iqaluit was the American military. Iqaluit, previously known as Frobisher Bay (named after the 16th Century English explorer, Martin Frobisher) was urbanized by the American military presence that began in the early 1950s. The American military built a large base here to prevent a Soviet attack from the north. The airbase, combined with the Distance Early Warning (DEW) Line stations across the north, brought wage labor and increased dependence on southern goods to the Arctic. With more people and more goods came more garbage, most of which was not biodegradable. Then, after the American's were "finished" with the north, they simply discarded their paraphernalia in piles outside of town, large Bulldozers, jeeps, and tons of assorted junk. For the Inuit, who were accustomed to garbage that was biodegradable, this new "junk" was unfamiliar. I think about this as I witness the current, messiness of Iqaluit. The Inuit, who learn best through example and imitation, did not have very good teachers.

Presently the town burns the garbage. There is considerable concern about the burning of garbage from many in the community. The ever-present sight of smoke in the distance, combined with occasional whiffs of toxic smells, makes one question the air quality in Iqaluit. Because Zoé hopes to measure the particle air pollution, she will need a scale. Yesterday we spent the afternoon looking for one that would measure milligrams. Fortunately, we found one at the Nunavut Research Institute.

Living in the Arctic has made us acutely aware of the impact that global pollution is having on residents of the Arctic. Pollution from the industrialized world travels to the Arctic in the northbound winds and ocean currents and gets trapped in the caribou and marine mammals. These animals are integral to the Inuit's ancestral diet. Sadly,

> *The bodies of Arctic people, particularly Greenland's Inuit contain the highest concentrations of industrial chemicals and pesticides found anywhere on Earth – levels so extreme that the breast milk and tissues of some Greenlanders could be classified as hazardous waist (Cone, 2004).*

Games, Sport, and the Environment

Many of those who play games and sport are far more likely to preserve and protect their natural world. They have learned a wholesome appreciation for fresh air, clean rivers and lakes, and un-muddled parklands. Like the Inuit, modern game and sport participants connect with their surroundings.

Games and sport have always been connected to our natural world. Their roots are set deep in our will to survive. The participants in games and sport provide hope that we can and will move forward. Moreover, it was our understanding and appreciation of the resources that made our survival possible that fashioned our positive associations with the natural world.

October 4, 2001

It is another snowy day in Iqaluit. The ravens, with their intense black feathers shimmering against the white snow, are more obvious than ever.

I woke-up last night thinking about modern athletes and their responsibilities as role models. I was actually thinking about Allen Iverson, the Philadelphia Seventy-Sixer's basketball guard who this past Monday said he would <u>not</u> be releasing his controversial rap CD. It was one year ago that the violent lyrics from his song "40 Bars" were seriously criticized. The words in the song were offensive to women, homosexuals, even parents.

> *Everybody stay fly*
> *Get money; kill and f___ bitches*
> *I'm hitting anything*
> *And planning on using my riches*
> *Down for zero digits*
> *I'm a giant, you're a midget*
> *Come to me with faggot tendencies*
> *You be sleeping where the maggots be…*

It was during my thoughts about Allen Iverson that I also thought about Arnold Schwarzenegger. The release of his latest film, *Collateral Damage*, has been postponed because the content was too closely related to the terrorist attacks on the United States. Like Allen Iverson, Arnold Schwarzenegger is a celebrated athlete. He won the "Mister Universe Title" three times and the "Mr. Olympia Title" seven times. Additionally, under former President George H. W. Bush he was the Official Spokesperson for, "The President's Council on Physical Fitness." Now a movie actor, Arnold Schwarzenegger is often referred to as, "The King" of motion picture violence. His last three films have had the following disclaimers:

> *Collateral Damage* – *"Terrorism and Violence"*
> *The 6th Day* – *"Strong Action Violence."*
> *End of Days* – *"Intense Violence and Gore."*

Inuit would not likely exhibit or sanction the demeaning and shameful behaviors of Iverson and Schwarzenegger. The Inuit had a profound understanding of their position as parents, teachers, and role models. They had been taught by those around them that any, less than ideal conduct, could not and therefore would not be tolerated. Their very survival depended on a wholehearted reverence for members of their clan and community. Any deviation from this design could lead to their total demise. As America begins to wake-up to the terror that exists in other parts of the world, might we also begin to think about the terror that exists in our own culture? America has been providing shelter to all sorts of behavior that is less than ideal. Again, our wake-up call is long overdue. Because modern games are a visible example of our collective ideology, participants have a responsibility to think critically about their roles and align these roles to protect and preserve our future. Modern game participants might wish to examine the life-world of the Inuit. After all, their practices provided near perfect harmony for hundreds of years.

Back To Transformation

This past week Elizabeth has been looking into the legacy of Inuit clothing. She and I have had many enlightening conversations about her discoveries. The Inuit's connections to the animals they hunted were obvious when you examine the spiritual, artistic and social traditions of their clothes. In the Inuit world, as was mentioned earlier, every living thing had a soul and a spirit. Furthermore, humans were integrated and aligned with all of nature. The clothing of the Inuit affirmed these connections. Using their superb know-how Inuit women created clothing that provided protection from the harsh elements and made visible the connections between animals and humans. By wearing clothing made from skin and fur, Inuit took on the form and personalities of animals. They visibly expressed their deep liaisons with the animal kingdom. Their clothing helped them connect with the strength, knowledge, and power of the animals' souls. In addition to the spiritual connections to their clothing, the Inuit also have deep connections to different helping spirits that guide and direct their lives. Often times they exhibited these spirits (amulets) on their clothing. One popular amulet for young hunters was a tiny pair of boots that they would wear on their backs. The tiny boots would assure young men of endurance and success on the land. In my studies of traditional games I always look for connections to modern games and sport. One obvious connection is clothing. Like the Inuit, modern game participants seek to "connect" through the clothing they wear. By donning Greg Norman (golf) shirts, Michael Jordan (basketball) shoes, Cal Ripken (baseball) jerseys, even the headscarves of Deon Sanders (football), they hope to transform themselves into the game heroes they admire.

I can feel and see the sunshine that has slowly driven away the clouds and snow. I think I will take a much-needed break and go for a walk on the land.

Religion in the Arctic

Emile Durkheim defined religion as, "A unified system of beliefs and practices relative to sacred things (Durkheim, 1982, p. 129).

From the beginning, Inuit were unified in their beliefs and practices relative to the Goddess Sedna, *Mother of the Sea,* their *Goddess of Life.* The animals she guarded were their lifeblood, their very means of survival.

> *Long Ago, there lived in the Arctic a young beautiful woman. Many men were presented to her as prospective husbands, but she rejected them all, until one day a handsome stranger came to her family's camp. He had many dogs and finely crafted hunting tools, and he promised her a life of comfort. She could not resist, and she left with him for his land across the sea, only to find on her arrival that she had been deceived. Her*

betrothed was in fact a seabird, and his dwelling was a hovel. When her father came to rescue her, they escaped in his boat across the calm sea. But her seabird husband's spirit, angered by this, pursued them and whipped the icy sea into a raging storm. In mid-ocean in a small boat, the father feared for his life and, to appease the bird, cast his daughter overboard into the wave tossed waters. But she clung relentlessly to the gunwale of his boat. Determined to release her grip, the father cut off her fingers at the first knuckle; the pieces fell into the sea and became ringed seals. Still she held on. Then he cut all her fingers at the second joint, and those pieces swam away as bearded seals. Other pieces of her fingers became walruses and whales. That is how seals were created, and that young woman became Nuliajuk, the Mother of the Sea, also known as Sedna. To this day, she lives at the bottom of the sea and controls all the animals in her watery domain (Pelly, 2001, p. 33).

It was said that when Inuit misbehaved or harmed their world, Sedna would get angry. In her anger her long hair would get tangled and trap the animals at the bottom of the ocean. This was Sedna's way of punishing Inuit who exhibited less than ideal behavior. The only path to redemption was for a shaman to travel to her world, untangle her hair and free the animals.

As I look around our world both here and abroad, it seems that Sedna and the Woman/Goddess she represents have disappeared. The flood of men's voices and men's ways of knowing is overpowering, from "America's New War" to the manifesto of the churches here in Iqaluit. The disappearance of Sedna seems widespread, creating a global imbalance in government, the church, and education. Now more than ever we desperately need balance. We need a woman's voice, the voice of Sedna.

Recently Elizabeth and I have been reading Leonard Shlain's enlightening book, <u>The Alphabet Versus The Goddess</u>. I highly recommend this book, especially as we try to make sense of our disparate world. If you do choose to read this book, you may wish to start at the end and then sort through the remaining chapters. I recently wrote

Dr. Shlain, a surgeon in San Francisco, to share with him some of our experiences in the Arctic. He wrote back with the following, affirming response.

> *Dear John,*
>
> *Thanks for your incredibly thoughtful comments. I am presently in Europe on a speaking tour and will return at the end of October. Can't open any attach at this internet cafe I am using. By the way what is the area of your expertise and where in New England are you situated? I speak at various universities and might be in your neck of the woods and perhaps we could meet. Best LS. PS Suggest you read Jeffrey Mason's, <u>Why Elephants Weep</u>.*

In his book, Dr. Shlain makes a convincing case for better balance between the Goddess and God, i.e., the image and the word, the gatherer and the hunter, the nurturer and the killer. He says,

> *Goddess worship, feminine values, and women's power depend on the ubiquity of the image. God worship, masculine values, and men's domination of women are bound to the written word. Word and image, like masculine and feminine, are complimentary opposites. Whenever a culture elevates the written word at the expense of the image, patriarchy dominates (Shlain, p. 7).*

He bases his argument on the history of the written word and the effect that our allegiance to written words has had on creating and sustaining a world dominated by men. Dr. Shlain strengthens his case by sharing the latest studies into hemispheric brain research and the influence written words have had on strengthening the left hemisphere at the expense of the right.

> *Left = Word/God/Hunter/Killer*
> *Right = Image/Goddess/Gatherer/Nurturer*

The manifest domination of God over Goddess that Dr. Shlain discusses in his book did not exist with the Inuit. Over time they created a balanced playing field where the Goddess/Woman and God/Man were interdependent, even as their skills diverged. Now more than ever we need the women of the world to unravel the knots of Sedna's hair. We need better balance between the God and the Goddess. As one woman said, women must, "...Lift their heads, raise their voices, dare to dream. The fire inside of us is our life, our light. We each have that fire within us and together we can keep it alive (*Keepers of the Fire*)."

Religion – Games and Sport

All of the world's major religions have the following characteristics: They celebrate sacred times in sacred places; they have faith in power/s not in their control; they have sacred leaders with "special" powers; there is fellowship, i.e., a unified system; and, there is always a "special" relationship with nature and the environment.

Sacred Times in the Arctic

In the Arctic Inuit often gathered to observe seasonal changes and personal events. One very important time was winter solstice.

> *The sun disappears at the winter solstice, emerging after ten days' absence in mid-January. Then, around noon, a shred of light shines on the southern ice horizon and fades immediately. An important ritual marked this instant. Soon after solstice, umialiks awaited the first sunrise of the season. The men rose early. But instead of walking out to hunt they were joined by their wives on the roofs of their uglus. With parka hoods raised against the wind they stood facing south. Dark blue, Imnat jabbed the horizon. As though breaching from the sea-ice, the sun would rise there. The first to greet it, catch it with their joy cry (Lowenstein, p. 128).*

Personal achievements such as the first kill of an animal by a young man or the first piece of sewing by a young girl were also important times.

> *When a boy catches his first seal, and has returned home with it, he will give gifts of meat to every household in his community, and his parents invite people to their home for coffee and cake, and to taste the meat of the seal (Nuttall, p. 37).*

Sacred Places in the Arctic

In addition to their sacrosanct respect for the land (Sacred Place), Inuit had respect for other sacred places as well. One special place was the large ceremonial snow house called the *qaggiq*. Many sacred activities, including healing, commemoration of achievements, and prayers of hope during hard times took place in the qaggiq. The local shaman led these activities, which often included song and drum dancing.

> *In a darkened iglu, a world within a world was created. A symbolic, glistening celestial dome over them, a floor cold and flat, like the iced-over sea, the sleeping platform representing mountains, the spherical glow of the qullig's flame like the moon's illumination in winter. In this world, the Inuit would be joined by the good spirits and by the tupilait (mythical or spiritual creatures), and by the animals of the sea and by the animals of the land. Nature was also there: they could hear the wind, the ice crackling and the thunder roaring; they could feel the snow storms and be blinded by fog (Saladin d'Anglure, p. 227).*

Faith in Powers Not in Their Control

For Inuit there has always been respect for powers not in their control. These mystical and supernatural powers were controlled by invisible rulers known as *Tuurngait*.

> *Tuurngag – a benevolent spirit, a kind of protecting genie or guardian angel, more or less powerful or wise, that a shaman*

consults by means of incantations to avoid illness, to heal, or to succeed when hunting (Saladin d' Anglure, p. 212).

Sacred People with Special Powers

For Inuit the shaman was fundamental to their culture. All of the forces of the universe passed through the shaman, who with his special powers of communication, passed them onto his audience. Once the mood was set, the shaman could obtain help from the spirits and reestablish a harmonious relationship between the different constituents of the world. Their powers and their ceremonies gave explanation to the world; they helped the Inuit understand their life and situations that, without their intervention, would have remained an uncomfortable mystery (Saladin d' Anglure, p. 227).

Connection to Nature

Earlier I shared the Inuit's beliefs regarding transformation. Their transformative beliefs worked with all of nature including other human beings. For example, when a child was born there was already a name waiting for them. One who had died had left behind his or her name, waiting for a new life.

Among us, as I have already explained to you, all is bound up with the Earth we live on and our life here; and it would be even more incomprehensible, even more unreasonable, if, after a life short or long, of happy days or of suffering and misery, we were then to cease altogether from existence. What we have heard about the soul shows us that the life of men and beasts does not end with death. When at the end of life we draw our last breath, that is not the end. We awake to consciousness again, and all this is effected through the medium of the soul. Therefore it is, that we regard the soul as the greatest and most incomprehensible of all (Saladin d' Anglure, p. 201).

As you think about all of the above please try to connect their place with your own religion. As I said earlier, these characteristics are common to all religions. And, since I am writing about games and sport, think about each of them in relationship to modern games or sport. You will plainly see that each can be satisfied by the phenomenon of games or sport. In games and sport you have:

Sacred Times – *Olympics, Worldcup, Superbowl, March Madness, Wimbledon…*

Sacred Places – *Olympia (Greece), Fenway Park (Boston Baseball), The "Big House" (University of Michigan Football Stadium)…*

Faith In Powers Not In Their Control – *The "Hail Mary Catch," The "Perfect Game," Injuries, Unpredictable Weather…*

Sacred People with Special Powers – *Pele, Michael Jordan, Tiger Woods, & Mia Hamm…*

Nature – *Sun (Light), Rivers (Kayaking), Lakes (Fishing), Oceans, Wind (Sailing), Ice (Skating), Snow (Skiing), Trees (Baseball Bats), Grass (Fields), and Animals (Leather Balls).*

Like the life-world of the Inuit, the phenomenon of modern games and sport are closely tied to religion. What has been part of the human fabric for thousands of years may simply be too hard to erase or expunge. Modern humans are simply not aware of the connections between religion and, games and sport.

Nature and "Messiness"

I often find myself returning to nature as I study, live through, and reflect on the north. Might the "messiness" of our modern world be tied to the disconnection or distance between humans and their environment? Philosopher Bruce Wilshire in his book <u>Wild Hunger</u> says that, "messiness" can often be related to the lack of human connections to nature. He writes,

> *If we lose this contact habitually primal needs go unmet. We imagine immediate substitute gratification – caffeine, cigarettes, cocaine, mere sex... [but] they are counterfeits that lead to dependency and loss of self respect. Only in a whole world in which we lose ourselves competently and ecstatically can we be coherent and powerful (Wilshire, p. 64).*

Modern Sport: The Spectator and Nature

The rise of modern sport in America in the early 1900's brought with it a dramatic increase in the numbers of spectators. Rather than participants and spectators sharing roles, a characteristic of pre-modern sport, modern sport established a clear divide between playing and watching. The opportunities for people to connect personally with games and sport, especially as it related to nature, were far less. Today this disconnection is even greater with television. We have become a society infatuated with watching, not doing. Two years ago I made a conscious decision to do something about my own personal disconnection, especially as it related to watching professional sport. This decision was not easy considering that my major field of inquiry is sport philosophy and I am deeply passionate about the aesthetic (beauty) of sport. This being said, I began watching less and doing more. To my surprise, I was not any less of a person, in fact I was actually more. The more came from real meaningful connections. By moving away from unnatural associations I had additional time to connect with Elizabeth,

Zoé, Parker, friends, neighbors, our home, our gardens, food, personal art, and dance. My connections to others and my environment helped me create a greater nearness to my natural self. Connections such as the ones I discovered by withdrawing from televised sport have also been enhanced by our summer journeys to Bois Blanc Island in Lake Huron, Michigan. For the past fourteen years Elizabeth, myself, and now our children, have been creating a living space on this remote island. The island provides us with connections to the natural world that are very powerful. From the thick forests, to the assortment of plant and animal life (including rattlesnakes), to the untainted water, to the changing heavens, the island brings us very close to the Oneness we desire, a Oneness so important to traditional Inuit.

Hunting and Gathering to Modern Games and Sport: The Journey

For 2,990,000 (nearly three million) years, the scheme that advanced our evolution was the reciprocal balance between hunter/killer (men) and gatherer/nurturer (women). Basic human survival fashioned this balance. The exceptional biology of women required that they provide for and nurture the offspring while the men hunted and killed for meat. A woman's nurturing capabilities made leaving her offspring impossible. It was also impractical for her to bring crying, hungry babies on long hunting expeditions. Leonard Shlain reminds us that throughout most of our evolution, A tribe's survival was as dependent on the female's nurturing skills as on the hunter's daring. Ongoing generations of healthy children were as vital as a constant source of protein. A strong interdependence cemented the sexes together even as their skills diverged (Shlain, p. 15).He goes on to say that,

> Hunting demands "cold bloodedness" tinged with cruelty;
> nurturance requires emotional generosity combined with warmth.
> A hunter must maintain a singularity of purpose when focused
> on prey; a mother must keep a field awareness of all that is

going on around her. While scouting for edibles, she cradled her infant in the crook of her left arm and had to monitor constantly the activity of her other children, playing at the periphery of her vision and consciousness. She could rarely carry out a task without, at the same time, remaining vigilant. Failure to do so often meant the death of, or serious injury to, her offspring.

And,

Because of their different roles, evolution, in time, equipped men and women emotionally to respond differently to the same stimuli. This resulted in men and women having different perceptions of the world, survival strategies, styles of commitment, and ultimately, different ways of knowing: the way of the hunter/ killer and the way of the gatherer/nurturer. In accommodating these differences, nature redesigned the human nervous system, radically breaking with all that had gone before (Shlain, p. 15).

The aforesaid scheme provided near perfect synchronization for 99.9% of our evolution. Changes emerged when approximately ten thousand years ago humans realized that the seeds from a previous harvest could be planted in a contained area. Their new discovery allowed the tribe or clan to remain in one location. This realization was soon followed by the domestication of animals, specifically goats, which now could be fed and reared in a confined area. About domestication Dr. Shlain adds, "As the practice spread, the hunter's skill was no longer necessary to bring home the bacon; it was already home, gently rooting and multiplying in a corral (Shlain, p. 32)." Almost overnight these events (farming) dramatically changed our long history of nomadic living. With farming came new concepts of possession and the guardianship/defense of land. Farming also dramatically altered men's roles as hunter/killers. As farmers, men no longer had to demonstrate mental and physical virtuosity in stalking, hunting, and killing animals. New contests of courage emerged to satisfy men's physical and predatory impulses, i.e., warfare, games and sport.

Of farming, archaeologists have uncovered intriguing evidence that suggests that men in some early farming communities were actually quite peaceful and did not exhibit the predatory behavior so common amongst their male ancestors. Sifting through the artifacts of farming settlements the archaeologists did not discover instruments associated with fighting and warfare. One theory for these apparent non-violent attitudes is that the physicality that farming required satisfied their brute male desires. Unfortunately this aforesaid evidence of men's peacefulness was probably more an exception, not the rule. History overflows with evidence of men's fighting-to-the-death combativeness. Even as I write, men are satisfying this innate urge to stalk, hunt, and kill ("America's New War").

While the agriculture revolution redirected men's lives and their brutish desires, women's lives and desires remained relatively unchanged. Their first priority was still providing for and nurturing children. Partnering in the management/running of the farm followed this important, life-sustaining responsibility.

This new agricultural scheme and the contests and games that emerged from it remained relatively unchanged for the next ten thousand years. Most of the contests and games were a rehearsal for men's capabilities with weapons (war), hunting, and with the plow (farming). The next revolution that would significantly transform humans and their contests was industrial; folks moved from the farm to the city.

It is interesting to note that the contests (games and sport) we gravitate towards in these modern times are only one hundred-fifty (150) years old. Baseball, football, hockey, and basketball as we know them, all had their beginnings in a fifty-year period (1850-1900). Their rise in popularity mirrors our move from an agriculture society to an industrial society. Without the plow, that for ten thousand years yoked men's brutish needs, modern games and sport emerged to help satisfy their innate desires.

The evidence of modern games' and sport's deep connections to our evolutionary past is everywhere, from the animals represented in mascots, i.e., *Rams, Ravens, Timberwolves, Wolverines, Dolphins and Diamondbacks,* to deep connections to religion (see earlier journal entry), to our donning of the modern skins from sport contests, i.e., embossed jerseys, hats, shoes, and sweatpants, to the pre-game and post-game celebrations that continue to accompany human contests and games. Games and sport have always been linked to human survival. The knots tightly woven over nearly three million years of evolution can never be unraveled.

October 5, 2001

Today (Friday) is the start of a four-day weekend in Iqaluit. Monday is Canadian Thanksgiving and the schools arranged for teacher in-service workshops today so that the students have an extended weekend. If we were in the States we might have thought about going away to visit friends or relatives. Because Iqaluit is only three miles wide by five miles long, we cannot go very far. I am sure many local families will pack themselves into their canoes (long boats) and head-out to their campsites to hunt seals and caribou. We have been invited to a Potluck dinner on Saturday night. We are all looking forward to the event.

Aesthetics – The Nature of Beauty

There is no word in Inuktitut for art. I have spent a good part of the past two days thinking about this incredible truth. Art, as we understand it, was wholly connected to the life-world of the Inuit. They were connected to its various forms in ways that were so deep-rooted that words were not needed to describe its meaning or function.

The songs, carvings, clothing, tapestries, amulets (good-luck charms), and drum dancing of the Inuit were so much a part of their lives that they did not consider them separate from their existence, thus there was no need for a word to describe them. Having spent most of my life engaged in art (dance), I find this perception extraordinary. In fact, I am struggling with the words to even explain it. The first sentence of this paragraph says it best. There is no word in Inuktitut for art.

In previous journal entries I have written about the connections Inuit had to their traditional songs (throat singing). Inuit drum dancing was no different; it facilitated connections to the natural world. The drumming and dance served many purposes. It foretold the location of animals, guided hunters on the land, shared visibly the stories of departed persons or events, and provided entertainment during the cold, long winter nights. It also served to:

> *Make merriment to counteract the burdens of the mind.*
> *Worrying is not good, it causes the mind to deteriorate.*
> *Leading a better life must always be a personal goal, although*
> *it is a difficult one to achieve (Arna'naaq, p. 11).*

The drum (qulautik), like the songs, carvings and clothing of the Inuit, had special significance. The caribou skin stretched tightly over a wooden frame with a handle on one side, was another affirmation of the nearness the Inuit had to the world around them. The drumstick (katuk) was wrapped with a caribou skin thong to prevent the drum from making too much noise. Too much noise might actually be detrimental by frightening the animals away.

Going to a dance or music concert or visiting an art museum was not part of the Inuit's way of knowing and understanding beauty (aesthetics). For them, beauty was all around them and they were connected in ways almost unimaginable to us modern folks. Again, writing about this notion is difficult because in the act of writing (words) I feel I am somehow separating from that which I am trying to explain.

Like the Inuit, I think we have all entered into states of "aesthetic beauty." For Elizabeth and me great moments of aesthetic beauty are the creation of our children, our home and surroundings (both Manomet by the sea, and Bois Blanc Island), and our dance. These creations provide us with transformation, connection, ecstasy, paradise, bliss, and harmony. Moreover, they guide us towards wonderful states of being. In the future I will try my best to take another lesson from the Inuit and remove the word "art" from my vocabulary so that there is nothing that separates myself from the "Creations." In other words, I will no longer need a name or label for it to provide bliss... It simply, will be...

I do not know if the above made any sense to you whatsoever. On some unexplainable level it does make sense to me. Like the Inuit having no word for art, maybe I just do not have the words to make clear what I am feeling and thinking.

On a separate note, I was reminded recently that we were almost, "at the top of the world." Yes, we are closer than we have ever been and I must say that the view from "way up here" is Wonder-Filled.

What is most interesting about our journey to the Arctic is to learn about the life-world of the people we are living with and around. For example, one of the young women we met in our throat singing class lives with her mother, grandmother, two uncles, and younger sister in a small two-bedroom house. When Zoé asked her about her father and what he does she said, "He lays in the graveyard." Even though her father is deceased, he is still doing something. He is lying in the cemetery. Her statement reminded me of the poem/prayer that was given to me when my father died (Chapter VI).

This young woman represents the future for Inuit. She has somehow been able to pull herself through the challenges that face many young people in the Canadian Arctic. She is the granddaughter of Inuit who were relocated from their communities and forced by the Canadian Government into residential schools. She is the granddaughter of Inuit who were poisoned with diseases and addictions of European marketers. Even her grandparent's dogs, their means of transportation and thus survival, were taken away and killed by the government. Despite all of this, the young woman still has a passion and enthusiasm for the future.

October 7, 2001

It is Sunday morning in Iqaluit. I woke up with a bit of a headache, the result of too much fun at the pot-luck.

Last night we were invited to a potluck supper by Susan Sammons and her husband Peter Kusugak. Susan is qallunaat and Peter is Inuit. Susan is the Director of the Language and Culture Program at Nunavut Arctic College. Peter works in Land Management for the Government of Nunavut. They and their two beautiful children live in a neighborhood called Happy Valley. I wonder if the name of their neighborhood had anything to do with the fun we had at their home.

Their house is quite magnificent. The inside is filled with many beautiful carvings (sanannguagag), and wall hangings. One entire wall was covered with the head and skin of a large polar bear (nanug). When we entered the family room we immediately noticed several large pieces of cardboard spread out on the floor supporting raw frozen caribou, muttuk (whale skin), and arctic char. Scattered amongst the meats were several ulu knives. On two tables nearby were caribou meatballs, veggies, and a carved turkey with stuffing, mashed potatoes, and gravy. Complimenting all of this was an assortment of delicious salads, breads, desserts, and libations brought by the invited guests. Elizabeth made two cakes, one chocolate and one pumpkin. Peter explained to us that in their home, "Inuit and White eat together, we do not separate the food." The Inuit are sometimes hesitant to eat traditional foods in the presence of qallunaat. This hesitation dates back to the early missionaries who tried to brainwash the Inuit into thinking that their diets and eating habits were primitive and barbaric.

Susan and Peter's party was a convincing affirmation of our capabilities for coexistence. Their guests were a wonderful mix of qallunaat and Inuit. Amongst the group were mixed marriages, common-law marriages, and adopted children. The collective unity of the group was heightened by our sharing (potluck), and dining together.

It seems that some of our greatest moments of connection in the Arctic have come while we were breaking bread with others. Food it seems is a wonderful medium for developing associations. Last night for example, I was taught how to use the ulu to shave sections off the frozen fish and caribou, eat them raw, all the while looking over my plate of turkey and mashed potatoes. Simultaneously, I was connected to two worlds. The feeling and tastes were scrumptious.

The realization that food has been one of the most effective mediums in the Arctic for facilitating connections, made me think about how important it is that we provide opportunities for different cultures to have meals together. This realization then led me to think about food in the Arctic and the large numbers of Inuit, adults and children, who go to bed hungry and undernourished. How can we hope to build a sturdy bridge when the very foundation of the bridge is weak due to undernourishment? What's more, I also thought about the fact that one professional baseball player's salary in the United States would pay for nutritious meals for every resident, approximately 28,000, in the entire Territory of Nunavut for one year. America! Where are our priorities? How can we break bread together when someone has ALL of the bread?

<u>October 22, 2001</u>

Yesterday (Sunday) was a reflective and poignant day.

For the past twenty years I have worked extensively with competitive figure skaters and coaches. My work has primarily been in the areas of off-ice dance and choreography. The success of this work has taken me to the finest skating centers throughout North America and to the past two Winter Olympics. In addition to hundreds of young amateur skaters, I have worked with champion skaters such as Peter and Kitty Carruthers (Silver Medal, 1984 Olympics), Jill Watson and Peter Oppegard (Bronze Medal, 1988 Calgary), and Todd Eldredge (United States and World Champion), to name a few. One highpoint of my work was being hired in 1995 to coordinate a week-long training camp for the top forty figure skaters in Canada, i.e., Elvis Stojko, ShaeLynn Bourne, Victor Kratz, etc. Unbelievably, I accomplished all of this as a non-skater, off the ice.

Forty years ago this week, I was a skinny, eight year-old boy in Fair Oaks, California who had been invited to a birthday party at the only ice skating rink in town. I remember putting on rental skates and trying my hardest to find my way, anyway, on the ice. Leading the birthday festivities was a skating teacher dressed in a black witch, Halloween costume. My skates were awkward and wobbly, I was freezing cold, and I fell so often that my clothes were soaking wet. It was a horrifying experience. Before yesterday, this haunting event was the one and only time I had ever worn ice skates and skated on ice.

For the past twenty years when skating students asked me to skate I would tell them that if they saw me skate, they might not want me to teach them dance or help them with their choreography. Little did they know, this was true because I really could <u>not</u> skate. Secretly however, I had an urge to be like them, to dance on blades, wind at my face, exploring an endless repertoire of human movement. At times I felt like a double agent, someone the skaters respected and trusted, yet someone who had not transformed himself into their world. Yesterday in the Arctic, this/that all changed.

One silent goal I had in coming to the Arctic was to learn how to ice skate. Sadly, for the past twenty years I have had a sense of self that simply could not bear to bare my skating vulnerabilities. I was afraid. I felt that by exposing my athletic weaknesses I would somehow not live up to the expectations of those that I was teaching. I even avoided friendly recreational skating opportunities on the ice rink that our neighbor had built in their backyard. Rather than face my fears, I simply avoided them, using all sorts of lame excuses.

In my plans for our sabbatical I thought that maybe the Arctic, being so far away from anyone and any organization that I had been affiliated with, would provide a perfect opportunity for deliverance. As part of my therapy, I even brought a new pair of figure skates in my luggage.

Both of Iqaluit's two skating rinks officially opened this past Friday. I had already stopped by the rink near our home and obtained the schedule for public and family skating. I had even worn my new figure skates and skate guards around our house trying desperately to break them in. Unfortunately, the skates I brought were a lost cause, they were simply too small. One thing I have learned in my twenty years of coaching skaters is that good, comfortable fitting skates are a must.

Yesterday afternoon Zoé said, "Dad, our family is going ice skating." At first I hesitated saying I was busy with my writing. My anxiety was still present. Zoé would have nothing to do with my excuse and insisted that I get ready to go. She, Elizabeth and Parker had already checked out the rink and said there were only a handful of people skating and they had rental skates in my size. Still a bit frightened I said to myself, "It is now or never." As our family walked to the ice rink I had all sorts of scary images. What if I fell and cracked open my head? The med-flight to Ottawa is fourteen thousand dollars ($14,000.00). Is this really the right time to face my vulnerabilities? With Elizabeth, Zoé and Parker cheering me on, I entered the blue doors of the arena.

In the skate rental area I found the only pair of skates that might fit my feet, a size twelve (12) pair of hockey skates, one without a shoelace. I found a loose black lace; the other skate had a white one, and laced both up tight. Then slowly, I inched my way towards the skating surface, carefully stepped onto the ice, and held tight the glass atop the boards. I had taken the first steps towards my rite of passage. One week away from my forty-ninth (49) birthday and I finally faced the challenge I have feared for the past twenty years. Simultaneously images of Inuit transformation, Inuit reciprocity, and Sedna (Elizabeth) washed over me as I began to glide over the Arctic ice. I had taken the first step towards what will become, I hope, a journey to freedom, freedom of movement, freedom of spirit, freedom from fear. Many have said that the most difficult step one takes towards anything important is the first step. Yesterday I took that first step.

To my surprise, I did quite well. I was quickly able to let go of the boards and skate. Knees bent, one foot in front of the other, round and round, I went. All of the terms, phrases, and corrections I had heard from skating coaches throughout the years circled like a raven in my head, inside edge, outside edge, three-turn, rocker turn… For the next ninety minutes I circled the ice rink, always traveling in the same direction, head up, all the while keeping a safe distance from the dozen or so other skaters. With smiles on their faces Zoé and Parker sped by me as they shared my joy. It was ecstasy of the highest order. I cannot wait until Wednesday (the Rink is closed Monday and Tuesday) when I can go again and continue to refine my skills; physical, mental, and spiritual. Oh, the *Wonders* of Play.

October 30, 2001

My Birthday! I begin today filled with the joy for life that Elizabeth, Zoé and Parker share. I also celebrate this day in a place far away, a place filled with wondrous lessons. Many of the birthday gifts I have received speak to the uniqueness of our journey to the Arctic, an igloo made from rice- crispy bars, a sealskin hanging, a promise of a sealskin vest, and a new pair of winter gloves.

I also begin this day with heartfelt concern for what is going on in our world. Our voices echoing from the north seem somewhat trivial in determining America's collective path. Our present location at the "top of the world," in another country, gives us a vantage point unlike many who are creating the current course of events. My sense of triviality reminds me of my birthday thirty years ago when I received my first draft notice to go to fight the war in Vietnam. I had avoided this calling because I was in college and maintained passing grades in twelve hours of class credit. Because my grades in one class began to slip, I decided to drop the class, signaling the United States Government, who immediately issued my notification to be drafted into the military. Prior to this I, with several friends, had been out spoken critics of America's involvement in this unreasonable and catastrophic conflict. Until President Nixon abolished the draft eighteen months later (July 1973), I was a frightened draft dodger. Now thirty years later, the tragic episodic memories of my past have reemerged. My sense of powerlessness is again present. I am however, still optimistic that our nurturing capabilities (Sedna) will rise up and provide some sort of balance to the killer force that seems to be so dominate. In a timely and appropriate birthday message my cousin Tom Kilbourn shared the following, *"Those not busy being born are busy dying" - E. E. Cummings.* Our journey to the Arctic is another example of our longing to continue the creation process.

I want to return to my previous entry on the deep relationships that exist between modern games and sport and traditional hunting. As I thought about the life-world of the Inuit, I realized that they did not experience an agricultural farming revolution. Because the geography of the Arctic does not favor farming, they were never yoked to a plow. Almost overnight they went from gathering, stalking, hunting, and killing to the industrial. In other words, in less than one hundred years they have had to make a transformation of hundreds of thousands of years of evolution. Is there any wonder that there might be some confusion swirling in the spirits of Inuit?

Always Moving – Moving All Ways

November 10, 2001

Everywhere in Iqaluit there is white snow made more obvious by the long dark days. Elizabeth and I have been very busy this past week teaching dance in the Physical Education classes at the Joamie Elementary School. The classes were kindergarten through grade five and the students were approximately seventy-five percent Inuit. We began each class with an uncomplicated dance warm-up followed by a simple line dance. Our goal was to have the entire school perform the warm-up and line dance during their morning assembly.

Each morning the students and staff of Joamie gather in the gymnasium for morning greetings and exercises. During the assemblies they honor birthdays and special achievements, sing songs, exercise, dance, and conclude with the singing of the Canadian National

Anthem. The anthem is divided into equal phrases of Inuktitut, French and English. Joamie principal David Serkoak leads the communal gathering of students and staff. In addition to being a terrific school leader, David is also an accomplished Inuit Drum Dancer. The wholesome tone set during the morning gathering permeates the atmosphere of the school.

Principal David Serkoak also leads a weekly Drum Dancing Club for Joamie students. The club meets each Wednesday during the lunch period. Each Wednesday, interested students bring a lunch from home so that they can stay at school and practice their drum dancing. During our time in Iqaluit we have attended several club meetings. With David as our inspirational teacher we have learned about, and practiced drum dancing with the young students. David explained to us that each person's dance with the drum is unique to their personality. He said, "Your dance is your story." He also said that as you move, your goal is to become, "one" with the drum. Traveling/loco-motor type movements are somewhat restricted as traditionally you would have been in an ice house/igloo with limited space.

Our time at the Joamie School was another affirmation of the "Positive Power" of dance. Moreover, like our early lessons in throat singing, it affirmed the importance of learning through experience. Our feelings of joy were very obvious when we all performed together at the Joamie School on Thursday morning, our final day.

Dance is a universal language. With and through dance, holistic interaction takes place regardless of one's ethnic heritage, language, gender, or socio-economic status. In addition, the physical challenges inherent in dance help facilitate wellness and promote creative strategies for learning. All of these were obvious as we witnessed the excited spirits of the Joamie students. Many of the children were actually sweating from the effort they put forward to master and perform their dance sequences. From our experiences at the Joamie school it was obvious that dance education can provide a meaningful path to harmonious success and happiness.

This last week we also shared our expertise in dance with the Iqaluit Dance Club. The dance club which practices social/ballroom dance, has been in existence for approximately one year, and meets twice weekly at the Catholic Parish Hall. One of the organizers of the club had heard that we were in town and called to see if we would be willing to teach one or more classes. We agreed and began on Thursday, November 1st.

Like our classes at the Joamie School, our teaching for the Dance Club was extremely gratifying. It was obvious from the start that we had plenty to teach the eager students, a nice mix of folks from many ethnic heritages. As I stated previously, the language of dance does not favor any one person or group. It is a wonderful facilitator for building bridges between disparate folks. The rewards from participation are numerous, regardless of one's age or ethnic heritage.

What has been most affirming about our work in dance at the Joamie School and at the Iqaluit Dance Club is how well it was received. Of our many talents, it seems that our capabilities as teachers and performers of dance is what is most valued and respected. Our classes also reaffirmed the need and appreciation people have for "moving" with others towards a common goal. The bonds created are deep, personal, and long lasting. For example, now when we see our students (young or old) in and around town, they greet us almost as if we were kin. On one level we are as we have experienced the closeness and heartfelt genuine-ness of each person's spirit. Does this deep need to "move," and be "moved" by others, have anything to do with our evolutionary past? I posit that our need to move is tightly woven and difficult to unravel from our individual and collective spirits.

<u>November 27, 2001</u>

I came to the Canadian Arctic to better understand the relationships between Inuit games, and modern games and sport. Towards this end I was fortunate to be able to record an interview with Alex Ameralik, a prominent Inuit athlete and coach. Alex Ameralik has been playing and coaching Inuit Games for the past twenty years. He has also attended every Inuit Summer Games in the Kitikmeot region. He was in Iqaluit attending the trials for the Arctic Winter Games. What follows is the text of his interview.

Question - *You are somewhat of an expert on how the games work?*

Alex - I am not an expert at it but I can tell. I can coach athletes to be better at what they are trying to accomplish. Set their goals. It is not all about competing against other people but trying to help them get better as an individual. I think of these games as individual sports, not team sports. I try to focus on one person, to get them better at the games.

Q - So you watch what they do and offer suggestions? They appreciate that?

A - Oh Yeah! I have helped a lot of guys over the years. Some I have never seen again and some come back for games. I think overall, all of the athletes I have seen have done pretty well.

Q - What keeps you coming back to compete in the games?

A - Meeting people, meeting different people, competing, having fun. That's it.

Q - You do not see too many other older guys trying out for the Nunavut Team?

A - I have always liked sports, all kinds of sports, team sports and individual sports. Overall, I think Arctic Sports are the most I like. Get to travel, see other people, meet other people.

Q - Is there a cultural aspect to why you like doing and teaching Arctic Sports?

A - I like it because on a cultural basis it's from our past, it's been done a long time ago and I try to pass it on to the next generation. And try to teach them how they did the games. Over the years a lot of rules have been changed. Some games have been modified for the better of the sport.

Q - Is this your contribution to the continuation of the games?

A - Yeah, Yes. I like to contribute to these games, help out the athletes and help out the judges. Give them ideas about which way would be better.

Q - How do you measure-up physically to these young guys?

A - Right now I am bad, out of shape (laughs). These young athletes are in pretty good shape, better shape than I am. That's for sure. I can tell in these sports here.

Q - When you were younger what was your favorite event. What were you best at?

A - The Alaskan High Kick. I can go right up there (motions to a height above his head). I cannot do it anymore. Got to do lots of exercise.

Q - Would you say Arctic Sports are growing?

A - Yeah. I think it is growing. I see a lot more athletes coming to Territorials (regional competition). When we have Territorials over the past two years I see more and more athletes coming to the Territorials. That's good. I think that's good. It tells me that more young guys are more interested in sports. More challenging.

Q - Why do you think it is important for the young guys to do sport?

A - It's a change from staying in one community for a long time. To get out and go to another community. Get a feeling for what the other communities are. It will help athletes in the long run that they compete against other people from other communities.

Q - How has it benefited you personally?

A - A lot of ways. It has benefited me a lot of ways. It has helped me in my coaching of younger kids. I learn more from different athletes around. It has helped me a lot, to be a better person towards other people. To understand other people more from different communities, different cultures. It's going to help me in the long run, helping other kids (CBC Radio).

In his interview Alex affirmed the importance of camaraderie to Inuit. He also shared how important games and sport were to building bridges between people. As I wrote earlier, one of the many wonders of games and sport is how you can be almost any place and through games and sport, you can enter into a union with others. The bond is more penetrating than race, gender, socio-economic status, or religious conviction. Together through games and sport, disparate people can become one in belief and practice.

<u>November 30, 2001</u>

So important to our time in the Arctic have been the lessons we have learned from our children. Some of the most important lessons we have learned have been those associated with play, games, and sport. For example at Zoé's school, the Aqsarnitt Middle School, students actually learn about and practice traditional Inuit games as part of their physical education program. To be able to share and experience these lessons firsthand is why we came to the Arctic. Some of the traditional Inuit games we have experienced with students from Aqsarnitt Middle School include:

The Airplane – *Lying face down with arms stretched outwards, the player is lifted up by his ankles and wrists and carried. The player who can maintain the airplane position the longest wins._*

The Back Push – *Sit on floor with your back against your partner. With hands and feet on the floor, try to push your partner backwards.*

The Kneel Jump – *Kneel on floor with toes straight. Swing arms back. Launch your body up and out to a squatting position. The furthest distance wins.*

The Knucklehop – *The player lies face down on the floor and positions himself like doing push ups with his hands like fists, putting all the weight on the knuckles. Lifting up his legs off the floor the player bounces forward on his fists. The player who goes the furthest distance wins._*

The Legwrestle – *Partners lie down on the floor and lock arms around each other's elbows. Count to three and raise inside legs to lock around each others' at the knee, keeping the outside leg extended at all times. The player who pulls the other off his back wins.*

The Mouth Pull – *Two players stand beside each other and wrap their arms around each other's shoulder, hooking the index finger into the other's mouth. Each player pulls until the loser yields to the other.*

The Musk Ox Push – *With both players on their hand and knees, and heads bent down against each others' shoulders, they attempt to push each other forward out of a designated area. Hands must be kept on the floor._*

> *The Sitting Knuckle Pull* – *With partners sitting and facing each other, brace legs against partner, lock knuckles. Partners pull. The loser is the one who breaks his/her grip.*
>
> *(http://www.athropolis.com/news-upload/11-data/*

December 1, 2001

Each day it gets colder and colder in Iqaluit. Yesterday was negative 20 degrees Celsius with a wind-chill temperature of negative 32 degrees. Frobisher Bay is nearly frozen preventing any travel by boat or ship. No one dares venture out of doors without the appropriate clothing and footwear. The assortment of winter fashions is most interesting, from beautiful seal skin coats to Canada Goose down parkas.

As our journey begins to wind down I thought it might be appropriate to share one or two notable reflections from our voyage to the Arctic. I decided to put these reflections in the form of a letter. What follows is my letter to Iqaluit.

Dear Iqaluit,

It is with gratitude and appreciation that we write this letter to you and your citizens. For the past three and one half months we have resided with and amongst you. The lessons you have shared are deep and far reaching.

We came to the Arctic to better understand your world and to hopefully share this understanding with our world. Our first-hand experiences with you and your people will go along ways towards helping others in the United States understand the Arctic.

Many professors come north to enhance their understanding of the Arctic. Most come alone or with other colleagues who have similar interests. Our two most important colleagues are our children, Zoé (11 years) and Parker (6 years). They have added much to our journey. Through them we were able to gain valuable insights into education, recreation, and peer relationships. The experiences, knowledge, and additional questions we have as a result of our stay are numerous.

One topic continues to occupy much of my spirit as I think about our stay in Iqaluit and moreover, the future success of Nunavut. That topic is *Bridge Building*, bridges between traditional and modern (including games), and Inuit and non-Inuit. Simply stated, what is required to construct meaningful bridges over which folks may pass successfully into the Twenty-First Century? Much of my research focused on this question.

As I wrote in earlier journal entries I feel strongly that the most meaningful bridges will be constructed through experiential teaching and learning that looks back and pushes forward. As Hany Geiogamah, Co-Artistic Director of the American Indian Dance Theatre, and Professor of Film, Television, and American Indian Studies at UCLA says,

> *We could do our beautiful traditional dances forever. But that's not what the Dance Theatre was formed to do. From the beginning, it was always to look for the possibilities and opportunities to take it to another step. We had to move carefully and conservatively and not be reckless or too frivolous in a direction of new creativity. That's how our culture works. It takes time to do this (Geiogamah).*

One important lesson that I have learned in the Arctic is that new possibilities and opportunities will continue to emerge from the essentials of culture, essentials that have defined societies from the beginning of human evolution. These essentials are people's belief in something greater than themselves and their affirmation and embodiment of these beliefs through human expression. In other worlds, Theology (nature of God), Aesthetics (nature of Beauty/Art), and Epistemology (how we know and understand).

Many seemingly separate, yet interconnected institutions, including government, education, the church, and the arts, will determine our success. New and creative paths leading towards the inclusion of the past with a vision of the future must be honored and embraced. For example, the notion of the Christian God as being, "The only good, there is no other God" (a quote from a leading Anglican Priest in the Arctic), must be broadened to include other forms of spirituality. One of the great lessons we have learned from our journey to the Arctic is that erasing or discarding deep longstanding beliefs can actually create more hurt than good. A more honorable approach is the one illustrated with stones by an Inuit elder at the conclusion of the documentary *Nuliajuk.* The elder says,

> *This represents the true Inuit way we used to live. I remember clearly the arrival of Christianity. I was moved to this place with an unstable foundation. I made up my mind without understanding – just believing…and wanting to follow it. My life became very unstable, I had no solid base. We want to get rid of this. From now on let us live like this. This represents white people and Inuit together. If we combined the best of the two, I'm sure we would have a great life. We'd really be helping each other (Nuliajuk/Film-Video).*

The expression of one's beliefs and feelings is an important part of a foundation that can lead to meaningful bridges. Human expression is shared best through music, drama, fine arts, dance, and games. During our stay in Iqaluit we have seen many magnificent examples of individuals who are creating opportunities for the aforementioned expressions. Some examples that we have experienced are David Serkoak's Drum Dancing Club, The Aqsarniik Middle School Youth Choir, John Huston's documentary *Nuliajuk*, Beth McKenty's Art for Youth, the Fine Arts Program at the Nunavut Arctic College, the Elder's Throat Singing Workshop sponsored by the Arctic Winter Games, the practice of Inuit games at the Aqsarniit Middle School, and many local carvers in and around our home, to name a few. During our stay we have tried to add to these efforts with our teaching of dance at the Joamie School and the Iqaluit Dance Club.

Music, dance, visual arts, film and games can be powerful pathways to understanding our complex world. They help us to know and understand the varied circumstances of the human condition by engaging our personal biographies with others unlike ourselves. They can provide strong foundations for bridges between disparate people. To my knowledge there has never been a culture of folks anywhere in the world that did not have an appreciation for such expressions.

There are many folks in Iqaluit who we would like to thank for helping make this a Life-Enriching journey. These folks include, Bruce Rigby, Susan Sammons & Peter Kusugak, Mary & David Wilman, David & Leslie Serkoak, Mary Ellen Thomas, Ron & Carol McLean, Caroline Cournoyer & the Elder Throat Singers from Quebec, Peter Geikie, Renata Solski, Diane Dennison, John Mathews, Keesa Nowdlak, Gayle Reddick & Zinour Fathoullin, the Iqaluit Dance Club, and the resourceful librarians at Nunavut Arctic College and Iqaluit Centennial.

In addition to these new friends we would like to thank the many outstanding young people who have been so important to our understanding of the Arctic. You are the future. Take the wisdom that has been shared with you, and like those that came before, move forward with dignity and grace.

In Unity of New Friends, Nakurmiik,

John Kilbourne & Family

On Endurance

Our extraordinary journey to the Arctic is slowly starting to wind down. We will depart ten days from today. As we get closer to our return date many of our experiences are once again washing over our spirits. The episodes of our journey are deep and enduring.

This past Sunday we spent the afternoon with our neighbor, his wife, and one of their three young sons. They are the Alainga Family, Pitseolak, Kootoo, and boys. On my first visit to Iqaluit I had been told about Pitseolak and his incredible survival story. I only discovered a short while ago that he actually lived next door to our home. What follows is Pitseolak's story, retold to the best of my capability. Because the human magnitude of the story is so profound I felt awkward asking Pitseolak if I could record our conversation. The personal connections that are possible through "lived" storytelling may have been less meaningful knowing that a recording was taking place. I am deeply grateful to Pitseolak for sharing such a heartbreaking event. Our time together was definitely one of the highpoints of our journey. I have supplemented what Pitseolak shared with information I obtained from the archives of local newspapers.

The Enduring Spirit of the Arctic

Simonie Alainga was a living Inuksuk in the town of Iqlauit. His wisdom about life guided many. Simonie's superb experience and knowledge about the land and sea was only surpassed by his unending commitment to his family and community. Many have shared with me the efforts he put forward, especially during the Christmas Holidays, to bring festive happiness to the people of Iqaluit. Titus Alooloo, a long time friend said, "When you went into his (Simonie's) house in Iqaluit, you always saw Baffin people staying there because they felt comfortable, and they were also fed and there was always tea on the stove for anyone who came into Simonie's house" *(Nunatsiaq News, Nov. 4, 1994)*.

On Tuesday, October 25th, 1994, Simonie Alainga, his son Pitseolak and eight others, including Pitseolak's uncles, cousins and good friends, boarded Simonie's thirty-eight foot fishing boat the *Qaqsauq,* for a walrus hunt. They had planned to go a week earlier but were delayed by mechanical problems. Because they would travel nearly two hundred kilometers and be gone for several days, the boat was packed with food, sleeping necessities, ammunition, and fuel. Their first stop would be an outpost camp, a location two days from Iqaluit by boat. After unloading and reorganizing their provisions, the team of ten would then travel another seven to eight hours to Loks Land, their hunting spot near the mouth of Frobisher Bay. The fact that there were ten men in the hunting party had notable significance.

> *Among Stone Age peoples, a core-hunting group comprised approximately <u>ten</u> adult males in their prime. Modern society still depends on the cooperation of approximately ten adults, male or female, to accomplish major undertakings. There are ten soldiers in a platoon, eleven players on a football team, nine on a baseball team, twelve members on a jury, ten to twelve on a board of directors, and nine Supreme Court justices. Ten vigorous adults usually assure inspiration, leadership, cooperation, and purpose (Shlain, p. 32).*

The team of ten vigorous Inuit males set out on October 28th to hunt Aiviq (Walrus). Despite the rough and tumbling seas, their hunt went extremely well. It was not long before they had taken twelve walrus. Together they worked as a well-organized team; some were shooting, some were retrieving, some were skinning and butchering, while others helped to pilot *Qaqsauq.*

With the meat of twelve walrus stacked neatly aboard the boat, they began their journey back to Iqaluit on Saturday, October 29th. They made slow progress as the waters continued to tumble the boat and its passengers. For whatever reason, possibly the extra weight, possibly a mechanical malfunction, the boat began to take on water. The resourceful crew quickly fired-up a gasoline generator and hooked it up to a small water pump hoping to pump the water out of the boat's hold. At approximately 11 P.M. they sent a mayday distress signal to a nearby outpost camp at Gold Cove that their boat was taking on water. Each time they radioed they were uncertain if anyone heard their message as they never received a reply.

The water pump could not handle the volume of water so some of the men began a desperate attempt to get rid of the water with five gallon buckets. It was soon obvious that their efforts were not working so a decision was made to abandon the *Qaqsauq* and board the sixteen-foot canoe boat that they had brought along for the hunt. All ten men attempted to board the canoe. The icy water splattered the canoe, nearly capsizing the boat the moment they boarded. One large gush finally toppled the boat spilling all ten men into the rough and frigid waters of Frobisher Bay.

Wearing a green military winter parka with deep pockets, wind pants, kamiks (boots) tied below the knees, a baseball cap covered with a tuque (knitted winter hat), and seal skin mitts, Pitseolak suddenly found himself under water looking up. Billy Kownirk, wearing a floater suit, a one-piece survival outfit, was nearby. Pitseolak, realizing it was not time for him to die, somehow managed to swim to Billy and hang onto his floater suit. Together they made it back to what remained of the *Qaqsauq*. Billy pulled himself up onto a small section of the boat that was above water. Pitseolak asked Billy to help him climb aboard as well. Frightened and cold Billy said, "I have pulled myself up and you must do the same." Pitseolak gathered his inner strength and pulled himself up alongside Billy. Sharing a small piece of the boat, they began a desperate search for the other eight men, fathers, uncles, cousins, and close friends. They looked and looked for any sight of their lost relatives and companions. While they were looking they were both thinking of what they might have done differently to correct their terrible misfortune. Almost in unison they realized that if they were to survive they must look forward. At this point it would do them absolutely no good whatsoever to expend any energy on the past. All of their energy and much more would be needed for Pitseolak and Billy to survive.

For Pitseolak and Billy this was the beginning of a three-day passage. Their bodies, half-submerged in the icy waters of Frobisher Bay, clung desperately to the wreckage of the *Qaqsauq*.

For several hours their floating abode did not move. At one point they noticed several walrus nearby staring at them. The walrus were so close they could actually look into their eyes. Both Pitseolak and Billy were concerned that one may try to ram their floating raft. This they feared would certainly mean the end as the weight of the walrus would quickly sink what remained of the boat. The walrus according to Pitseolak, looked as though they were hugging each other by clasping their flippers. With one eye on the walrus they also noticed a group of seals nearby that the walrus politely avoided. This behavior seemed very peculiar, considering that walrus eat seals. Suddenly Pitseolak and Billy felt their floating abode begin to move. It was as if the walrus had swum underneath and were helping to direct them towards land. I asked Pitseolak if he thought the actions of the walrus were somehow connected to Sedna?

Pitseolak continued to pray throughout he and Billy's ordeal. It was through prayer that he found the will to live and the strength to endure. During Pitseolak's prayers his life from about the age of nine to the present flashed through his mind. He felt deep sorrow for all of the mistakes he had made and the anxiety he had caused others. He also felt deep love, deeper than ever before, for those near and dear to him, most especially his wife Kootoo. It was at this point in the story that the emotion of the account washed over Pitseolak and he began to cry. It was a moment in my life I will never forget. Pitseolak, an upright man, husband, father, accomplished hunter and provider to many, was cleansing the windows of his spirit with tears so that we may see our world anew. It was not long until tears began to flow from all of our eyes. At this point there was a long pause in the story to honor and celebrate our collective cleansing.

Pitseolak and Billy continued to cling to the remains of the *Qaqsauq*. Pitseolak kept dipping his lower legs and feet into the icy water to keep his blood circulating. His father had taught him that because salt water freezes at a lower temperature than fresh water, he needed to keep sloshing seawater in his boots to keep his feet from freezing. Both he and Billy were cold, thirsty, and hungry. Somehow despite the hardships, they endured.

Some Inuit elders believe that Pitseolak and Billy's will to live is linked to their duty to pass their story onto others.

> *It's an age-old Inuit tradition that whenever there is a tragedy there are survivors who live on and tell the stories of what happened. People live to pass on the experience for future generations. Somebody had to live to tell the story. Sometimes miracles do happen... There were a lot of prayers, and they were answered (Nunatsiaq News, Nov. 4, 1994).*

As word of the accident spread the search for the missing hunters intensified. There was a mass exodus of search teams. Two twin otters (airplanes), a Hercules jet, an Aurora aircraft, a Labrador helicopter, a Canadian helicopter, a department of Fisheries and Oceans boat, and a chartered fishing boat, all took off to look for their friends and fellow Canadian citizens.

On Monday it began to snow and a small amount began to accumulate on a section of the boat. The fresh snow provided a small amount of water and allowed Pitseolak and Billy to quench their thirst. Petseolak reminded Billy to let the snow melt in your mouth before you swallow. This was another lesson his father had taught him. It was during this time that they also began to hear the engine of an airplane overhead. Because of persistent low clouds and snow flurries however, the crew of the plane was unable to see the two floating survivors.

Also on Monday, with limited visibility, the search crews found debris floating in the rough seas near where the boat went missing. The *Qaqsauq's* cabin door, engine cover, and a piece of the wheelhouse were recovered. When night fell and none of the hunters had been found, the search efforts were called-off until first light Tuesday morning.

After nearly sixty hours, half submerged in icy waters and clinging to the remains of the *Qaqsauq*, Pitseolak remembered another lesson his father had taught him. He broke a small piece from the boat's glass windshield and placed it over the dark section of one of his sealskin mitts. His hope was that during a break in the cloud cover he could create a reflection from the sun that the plane's crew might spot. His plan worked. On Tuesday afternoon at 1:30 P.M. the crew of the Hercules aircraft spotted Pitseolak and Billy floating about sixteen kilometers from shore. A helicopter dropped a raft from overhead and guided it towards the two men. Once aboard the raft they were picked up by a fisheries and oceans vessel and taken to a nearby outpost camp. Both Pitseolak and Billy were conscious and talking when their rescuers arrived. They had continued to talk to one another during their entire three-day ordeal. Because of the extreme wet and cold their clothes were soaked clear through to the skin and their limbs were swollen. So swollen were their limbs that their clothing had to be cut off. From the outpost camp they were taken by helicopter to Baffin Regional Hospital in Iqaluit. Miraculously both Pitseolak and Billy somehow survived.

The outpouring of family and friends that gathered to honor the eight fallen comrades and the two survivors was unlike anything Iqaluit had ever witnessed. Hundreds of folks from throughout the north and from all walks of life gathered at St. Judes Anglican Cathedral, the nearby Parish Hall, and on the land outside.

> *Before the service began, the crowd inside the church remained silent. Some cast their eyes down in respect. Others stared blankly at the front of the church, where eight white, wooden crosses leaned against the altar. Minutes before the service began, the crowd in the church reception area parted and a young man in a wheelchair was escorted to the front of the congregation (Nunatsiaq News, Nov. 11, 1994).*

The young man was Pitseolak Alainga.

The bodies of the eight other Inuit hunters have never been found, Iola Nooshoota (21 years), Ooletoa Pishukte (24 years), Joepee Panipak (28 years), Kellypalik Pishukte (45 years), Sammujualie Kootoo (52 years), Eepeebee Peterloosie (56 years), Simonie Alainga (57 years), and Johnny Shoo (59 years).

As Pitseolak brought his heartbreaking retelling of the tragedy to a close he said that each time he tells the story he feels a little bit stronger. I then shared with him the deep appreciation we have for him telling our family the story.

December 10, 2001

Our final week in the Arctic begins today. We all have sad polar bear faces as we think about leaving this "special" place.

This past Saturday we had another polar bear eyes day. Susan Sammons and Peter Kusugak invited us out on the land on snow machines. There were a total of twelve folks who went on the outing, Susan and Peter and their two children, our family, Peter's brother and his girlfriend, and a graduate student (Laval University, "Inuit Religion") and her boyfriend. We boarded three snow machines (Skidoos), one pulling a large qamutik (sled) with a box attached, and one pulling a shorter qamutik with no box. Parker had the best seat as he rode in front of Peter and helped to pilot the largest skidoo. His polar bear eyes were bigger than life.

Our destination was Susan and Peter's small (10' x 12') cabin, ten kliks (kilometers) north of Iqaluit. The boyfriend and I rode on the smaller qamutik without any padding to cushion us or sideboards to keep us from falling off. Because there was not much snow the ride was bumpy and uneven. Actually it was far more treacherous than I had imagined. Fred (the boyfriend) and I hung on for our lives, at times being completely air born. My rear end is still so sore that I can hardly sit, especially on hard surfaces.

After about forty minutes of travel over frozen rivers and surrounding terrain we arrived at their cabin. As I told everyone when we arrived, "This is better than any roller coaster ride."

Several years ago Peter built their cabin as a permanent outpost camp. It is one of only two such cabins situated on the outskirts of Iqaluit. The cabin sits high on a hill overlooking a river, has a narrow loft for sleeping, three windows, a table, chairs, and a makeshift couch.

After taking in the spectacular scenery, we unloaded our picnic lunch while Peter fired-up the Coleman stove that he had brought in the qamutik. Peter and Susan's daughter Kukik, and Zoe fetched some snow for tea while others spread-out the picnic on the table inside. For the next two hours we shared food, conversation, and laughter, mostly inside the cabin. The cabin remained very cold despite some heat from the stove. The hot tea and assortment of food helped ease some of the chill.

As the sun began to set we packed up our belongings, loaded the qamutiks, and began the journey back to Iqaluit. I, for one, was not looking forward to another "Bucking Bronco" ride. With brave faces both Fred and I mounted our qamutik and our driver Nanuq (Peter & Susan's son), sped off across the snowy terrain.

Once home we unpacked, warmed-up our feet, and laid down in our cozy beds for a nap. Before we closed our eyes Parker said, "You know that picture of Peter and I on the skidoo? I want that one in my bedroom." With images of the magnificent Arctic floating in our heads, we were fast asleep.

On Saturday night we went to the local movie theatre at the Frobisher Inn. The new "Harry Potter" film had opened in Iqaluit the night before. It was a good thing that we had purchased tickets in advance, as the show was completely sold out. Fortunately for me, the seats were well cushioned.

Going to a movie in Iqaluit was very interesting. The owner of the theater does almost everything, from selling tickets to operating the projector. Prior to the start of the movie he walked through the theater and asked many young children if they could see the screen. And, during the show he asked me if the theatre temperature was ok. All the while the owner's two small dogs roamed through the theatre, occasionally rubbing up against our legs. It was "Community Movie Theater" at its best. The owner's courteous efforts, and the efforts of others like him in Iqaluit, will be missed. The film (Harry Potter) was also very good.

On Sunday we watched the award winning epic film, *Atanarjuat: The Fast Runner*. The film has not yet been released in the United States.

> *Widely considered a landmark in world cinema, "Atanarjuat The Fast Runner" is Canada's first feature-length fiction film written, produced, directed, and acted by Inuit in the Inuktitut language. A spectacular achievement from the award-winning production team at Igloolik Isuma Productions (Atanarjuat/Film-Video).*

Watching this incredible film was a fitting ending to our stay in the Arctic. The wisdom and hope demonstrated at the conclusion of the film, combined with the extraordinary talents of those who created the film, offer great hope for the Arctic and its people. Fortunately I was able to purchase a copy of the film to share with our friends and colleagues in the United States.

As our journey winds down all of our love and appreciation for this "special" place is becoming more apparent. The lessons we have learned about games and sport, and more importantly life, are deep and enduring. The more we learned the more all of us realized how much more there is to learn from our new friends in the Canadian Arctic.

The following letter that Zoé' wrote her teacher is a powerful tribute to what this journey has meant to all of us. She titled her letter, *You Have The Power!*

Dear Renata,

> *You were and always will be a great teacher. No one could replace you as a teacher. What I'll miss about you is how you took everyone's talents and used them somehow. You also grouped us in to groups according to our rates of learning so that we weren't struggling or falling asleep. It is going to be hard to go back to such a large school. I've experienced more than I ever could have in the United States. This culture taught me that sometimes, "Smaller is Better." Aqsarniit Middle School has almost become my "learning home." Despite some problems, I really loved your class. You and the whole staff understand everyone and even*

though there are some trouble makers I don't think I ever heard you yell. Your voices were stern but never "mean." This class has become so familiar to me that it will be hard to go back to my regular school.

Here are some "Thank You" gifts and the books. Please give them to some one or keep them. If you give them to a person, give them to someone less fortunate. But you may keep them as well.

Thank you Renata for a great 3 ¾ months in your class. I will never forget you. Love, Zoé Kilbourne
P.S. You have permission to share this with other staff or our class if you like.

WE WILL NEVER FORGET.

Tavvauvusi (Goodbye),
The Kilbourne Family

Epilogue

In *Chapter III, Exploring the Near at Hand,* Dr. Richard Nelson talks about an important lesson he learned from his teacher Catherine Attla. He says that Catherine, "points out constantly what little we know of this, what little we know of that (*RWZ*, p. 33)." He goes onto say that his written works are, "a kind of progress report: this is where I am now, recognizing that there will always be farther to go (*RWZ*, p.33)."

Running with Zoé is a progress report on where I am now in my understanding of play, games, and sport. Like Dr. Nelson, there will always be farther to go. There will always be another conversation. Stay tuned and thank you for listening...

References: *Running With Zoé*

Brown, Larry. Personal Interview, 1983.

Couch, Jean. "The Perfect Post Run Stretching Routine," *Runners World*; April 1979: 84.

Cooper, Donald L. MD. and Fair, Jeff. "Stretching Exercises for Flexibility," *The Physician and Sportsmedicine;* March 1977: 5, 114.

Cureton, Thomas K. "Flexibility As An Aspect of Physical Fitness," *Research Quarterly*; 1941: 381-390.

DeVries, Herbert A. "Evaluation of Static Stretching Procedures For Improvement of Flexibility," *Research Quarterly*; 1962: 479.

DeVries, Herbert A. "Electromyographic Observation of the Effects of Static Stretching Upon Muscular Distress," *Research Quarterly*; 1961: 479.

Erving, Julius. Personal Interview, 1983.

Graham, Martha. "A Modern Dancer's Primer for Action, "*Dance as a Theatre Art*; 1974: section 5, Selma Jeanne Cohen, ed; New York, 133-43.

Graham, Martha. "A Modern Dancer's Primer For Action, "*The Dance Anthology*; 1980: 45-6.

H'Doubler, Margaret N. *Dance: A Creative Art Experience*; 1957: University of Wisconsin Press.

Jacobson, Edmund. *You Must Relax;* 1934: New York.

Jesse, John P. "Misuse of Strength Development Programs," *The Physician and Sports Medicine*; Oct. 1979: 46.

Kirstein, Lincoln. "Dance A Short History of Classical Theatrical Dancing," *A Dance Horizons Republication*; 1935: 286.

Klafs, Carl and Arnheim, Daniel. *Modern Principles of Athletic Training*; 1977: St. Louis.

Langer, Suzanne. *Feeling and Form*; 1953: Scribners Sons, NY.

Kirshenbaum, Jerry. "Scorecard," *Sports Illustrated;* April 25, 1983.

Miller, William H. "Little Bill," *How to Relax: Scientific Body Control;* 1945: Smith and Durrell, NY.

O'Sullivan, Maria Parham. "Indians Stretch For Strength, "*The Physician and Sportsmedicine*; July, 1975: 109-110.

Reynolds, Gretchen. "Stretching the Truth," *New York Times;* Nov, 2, 2008.

Rolf, Ida. *Rolfing: The Integration of Human Structures*; 1977: Harper and Row, NY.

Schultz, Paul. "Flexibility: Day of the Static Stretch," *The Physician and Sportsmedicine*; Nov. 1979: 109.

Shirley, Bill. "Who Are The World's Best Athletes?," *Los Angeles Times*; Nov. 25, 1981.

Stingleman, Sue Ellen. *Conditioning for Dance: Master's Thesis*, U.C.L.A.; 1979.

Swanbom, Don. *Strength Off-season Conditioning Manual*; 1980: U.C.L.A.

Toney, Andrew. Interview, *ABC Sportsbeat*, 1983.

Wooden, John. *In Honor of John Wooden*, U.C.L.A. James West Alumni Center, Los Angeles, CA 1982.

References: *A Journey to the Canadian Arctic*

Arna'naaq, L. *Drumbeats of the Past.* Nunavut Arctic College, Iqaluit, Nunavut, 2001.

Brody, H. *The Other Side of Eden: Hunters, Farmers and the Shaping of the World.* New York: North Point Press, 2000.

Caras, R. *A Perfect Harmony: The Intertwining Lives of Animals and Humans Throughout History.* New York: Simon & Schuster, 1996.

Cardinal, H. *The Unjust Society: The Tragedy of Canada's Indians.* Seattle, WA: Univ. of Washington Press, 1999.

CBC Radio. Iqaluit, Nunavut, Nov. 10, 01.

Cone, M. (2004, Jan. 18). "Pollutants Drift North , Making Inuits' Traditional Diets Toxic," *Boston Globe,* p. A12.

Darwin, C. (2000). *On The Origin of Species.* Cambridge, Massachusetts: Harvard University Press.

Durkheim, E. (1982). *The Elementary Forms of Religious Life.*

Geiogamah, H. *Los Angeles Times,* Nov. 20, 2001.

Issenman, B. *Sinews of Survival.* Vancouver: Univ. of British Columbia Press, 1997.

Lowenstein, T. *Ancient Land: Sacred Whale.* New York: Farrar, Straus & Giroux, 1993.

Nunatsiaq News. Iqaluit, Nunavut XOA OHO. Nov. 4, 1994.

Nunatsiaq News. Iqaluit, Nunavut XOA OHO. Nov. 11, 1994

Nuttall , M. *Etudes/Inuit Studies*, 24[2]. 2000.

Pelly, D. *"Link Between Inuit and Seals," Above & Beyond.* Sept./Oct. 2001

Pelly, D. *Sacred Hunt.* Seattle, WA: Univ. of Washington Press, 2000.

Robinson, J. *"Real Travel," UTNE Reader.* Jul/Aug., 2001.

Saladin d'Anglure, B. *Interviewing Inuit Elders: Cosmology & Shamanism.* Iqaluit, Nunavut: Nunavut Arctic College, 2001.

Shlain, L. *The Alphabet Versus The Goddess.* New York: Viking, 1998.

Tungilik, V & Uyarasuk, R. *Inuit Perspectives on the 20th Century Transition to Christianity.* Iqaluit, Nunavut: Nunavut Arctic College, 1999.

Wallace, M. *The Inuksuk Book.* New York: Firefly Books, 1999.

White, L. *For God So Loved The World, UTNE Reader.* Jul/Aug., 2001.

Wilshire, B. *Honoring Our Hunger For The Ecstatic, UTNE Reader.* Sept/Oct., 2001.

References *(Film/Video)*

Atanarjuat: The Fast Runner. Isuma Distributing International, 2000.

Keepers Of The Fire. National Film Board of Canada.

Kitikmeot Drum Dancer. Les Productions Vic Pelletier, 1999. *Nuliajuk.* Triad Film Productions Ltd.

Netsilik Eskimos: People of the Seal. National Film Board of Canada, 1967.

Northern Games. Indian and Northern Affairs Council of Canada, 1980.

Nuliajuk. National Film Board of Canada.

References (Web Sites)

Inuit Games - http://www.athropolis.com/news-upload/11-data/

Appendix

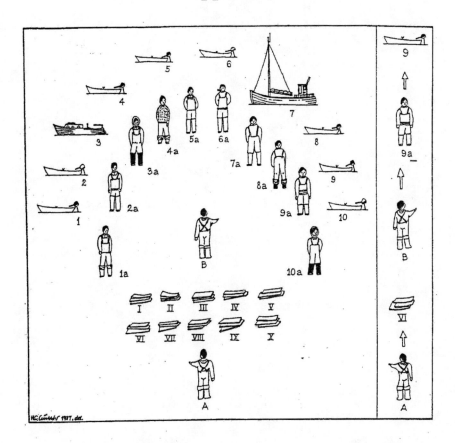

Sharing of "*mattak*" following a communal beluga hunt. Ten boats (1-10) have participated in the hunt, eight boats with outboard engines, one motorboat (3) and one fishing vessel (7). The "*mattak*" has been pooled and divided equally in ten shares (I-X). Posted in front of the piles of "*mattak*" is one hunter (1a-1oa) from each of the ten crews. Among the ten crews two persons (A and B) are selected to draw lots — both facing the ten crews. When A points at one of the piles of "*mattak*" (VI for example) he asks: "Who is going to have this pile?" Then B, who cannot see which pile is indicated, selects one of the ten (1a-1oa) hunters. Waiting until all ten piles have been allocated, all boat crews go and pick up their shares. When later sharing the meat, the same procedure is followed.

Etudes Inuit Studies, Vol. 13, No. 1, 1989, p.32

About the Author

Dr. Kilbourne has devoted nearly all of his adult life to helping individuals know and understand play, dance, games, and sport. His Bachelor's degree is in Creative Drama & Movement from California State University Long Beach. His Master's degree is from the University of California at Los Angeles in Dance Education with an emphasis in Dance & Sport. While at UCLA he served as Graduate Assistant (Basketball Conditioning) to then head coach Larry Brown. His Ph.D. is from The Ohio State University where he continued his work exploring the relationships between sport and performance. In 1982 John became the first full-time conditioning coach in the National Basketball Association with the Philadelphia Seventy Sixers. He helped them in the pursuit of their 1983 World Championship. In addition to his work in basketball, John has extensive experience in figure skating both in the United States and Canada. Presently he serves as a professor in the Department of Movement Science at Grand Valley State University in Allendale, Michigan.

John is a former member of The Margalit Dance Theatre, The Detroit Dance Collective, and presently co-directs with his wife Elizabeth, The Blau Rhino Dance Ensemble.

Dr. Kilbourne has won numerous awards including, The 2009 GVSU Distinguished Professor of the Year Nomination, The Commonwealth of Massachusetts Citation of Outstanding Performance, the 2004 Bridgewater State College Award for Academic Excellence, and the 2000 Massachusetts Association for Health, Physical Education, Recreation, and Dance Honor Award.

Dr. Kilbourne is a productive scholar having written numerous articles. He is a frequent guest speaker throughout North America. One of his current research interests is on the games of Arctic people. During the fall of 2001 he and his family moved to the Canadian Arctic where they experienced the culture and games of Canada's Inuit.

LaVergne, TN USA
25 August 2010
194659LV00003B/4/P